# THE RISE & FALL OF FALMOUTH JAMAICA

Carey Robinson

© 2007 by Carey Robinson
First Edition 2007
© 2011 by Carey Robinson
Second Edition 2011
10 9 8 7 6 5 4 3 2

All rights reserved. No part of this book may be reproduced, stored in a retrieval system, or transmitted, in any form or by any means, electronic, mechanical, photocopying, recording, or otherwise, without the prior written permission of the publisher(s) or author(s).

If you have bought this book without a cover you should be aware that it is "stolen" property. The publisher(s)/author(s) have not received any payment for the "stripped" book, if it is printed without their authorization.

All LMH titles, imprints and distributed lines are available at special quantity discounts for bulk purchases for sales promotion, premiums, fund-raising, educational or institutional use.

Cover Design: Susan Lee-Quee Design and Sanya Dockery
Typesetting: Michelle Mitchell, PAGE Services and Sanya Dockery
Executive Editors: Charles Moore and Kenisha T. Duff, LMH Publishing
       Julia Tan, Consultant

Published by: LMH Publishing Limited
Suite 10-11
Sagicor Industrial Park, 7 Norman Road
Kingston C.S.O., Jamaica
Tel: 876-938-0005;
Fax: 876-759-8752
Email: lmhbookpublishing@cwjamaica.com
Website: www.lmhpublishing.com

Printed in the U.S.A.                                    ISBN 978-976-8202-80-2

**NATIONAL LIBRARY OF JAMAICA CATALOGUING-IN-PUBLICATION DATA**

Robinson, Carey
    The rise and fall of Falmouth, Jamaica / Carey Robinson. – Rev. ed.

    p. : ill. ; cm
   Bibliography : p. - Includes index
   ISBN 978-976-8202-80-2 (pbk)

   1. Falmouth, Trelawny (Jamaica)    2. Jamaica – History
   I. Title

972.92    dc 22

*To my mother, Marion Robinson, who was born and raised in Falmouth and wanted to spend her last days there - but never made it.*

## ACKNOWLEDGEMENTS

The author extends grateful thanks to the following people:

The Fitz-Ritsons: who allowed their family papers and oral memories to be freely used.

Frederica (Moore) Gaynair: for tales of Dr. Vine and others.

The Lazarus sisters, Vera and Lally: for sharing their memories of Falmouth life.

The National Library of Jamaica for allowing the use of 'original' material.

Custos Roy Barrett: for the use of his notes on Falmouth's characters.

# Contents

Foreword

Introduction

The Birth of Trelawny and Falmouth .................. 1

Trelawny's Maroon War .................. 5

Falmouth Grows and Prospers .................. 14

The Barretts and Tharpes .................. 17

The Splendid Gentry .................. 28

The 55th And The French Scare .................. 32

The Trelawny Militia .................. 41

William Knibb & The Baptist War .................. 44

The End of Slavery .................. 52

The Black Blood Of Bleby .................. 55

The Maverick of the House of Reid .................. 58

A Fiery Editor .................. 68

Other Newspapers .................. 76

| | |
|---|---|
| Lively Times | 77 |
| Dangerous and Amazing Things | 89 |
| Social Unrest | 98 |
| Governor Eyre's Visit To Falmouth | 104 |
| Brightening The Dull Times | 109 |
| The Big Scandal of 1867 | 112 |
| Dr. Vine and Other Characters | 117 |
| WiIlliam Chin-See | 126 |
| The Courageous Knibb Sisters | 129 |
| The Silver Cup of Daniel O'Gilvie | 134 |
| The Poor House and Matron Marion | 138 |
| 'Classic' Charlie - The Shark Killer | 144 |
| The Ghost of Phillip Fitz-Ritson | 147 |
| The Court House Burns | 154 |
| Epilogue | 161 |
| Bibliography | 165 |
| Index | 167 |

# **FOREWORD**

## *The Rise and Fall of Falmouth, Jamaica*

The *Rise and Fall of Falmouth, Jamaica* is an attempt by writer, historian Carey Robinson, to record Falmouth's "hey days" from its founding in the late 18$^{th}$ Century to the start of the 20$^{th}$ Century, when the fire which almost destroyed the Falmouth Court house symbolized the death of colonialism and the emergence of a new Jamaica. It is a quick journey through the years.

The book recaptures some high points of the Maroon wars and conflicts with rebel slaves. For a brief period, the "Garrison town" of Falmouth boasted Jamaica's busiest harbour, with vessels arriving from England and Canada to drop off supplies and take on cargo. There are highlights of the nearly 700-strong 55$^{th}$ Regiment of foot, and the highly honoured and respected Trelawny Militia. The town played its role in the fight for freedom with the work of Methodist and Baptist missionaries such as John Rowe, Thomas Burchell, William Knibb and Henry Bleby. They suffered at the hands of the supporters of the pro-slavery Colonial Church Union and both their congregations and individual Church leaders were arrested and physically attacked.

Falmouth boasted its own newspaper which kept its citizens informed on politics, international news, interesting trivia, gossip and the disorderly behaviour that the town became known for. The social life of the citizens gives us an insight into some of the scandalous behaviour of the day, from nude bathing in the Martha Brae river to the eccentric and amusing behaviour of the town's characters. Visitors of all types, 'young dimpled rosy cheek ladies and full, matronly mamas and aunts accompanied by the big merchants, planters, lawyers and doctors', attending the popular annual horseraces and balls brought back the lively times to Falmouth following the aboliton of slavery. So did memorable characters: Daniel O'Gilvie, the Knibb sisters, Dr. Simeon Vine and William Fitz-Ritson...

The end to Falmouth's days of glory and the elaborate lifestyles of its gentry came with the fire which almost destroyed the most treasured showpiece — the court house, the heart and nerve centre of the town.

# INTRODUCTION

This is an intimate story of the town and people of Falmouth (capital of Trelawny) in their brief days of glory.

It begins in 1665, when Trelawny was part of the sprawling, new, "frontier" parish of St. James, on the north side of Jamaica.

The story moves rapidly through the perilous Maroon wars to the carving out of Trelawny from St. James, and, later the birth of Falmouth as the capital of the new parish.

Over one hundred sugar estates blossomed throughout Trelawny, worked by nearly twenty-eight thousand slaves. The parish boasted more slaves than any other. Ironically, it was also the place where the stubborn fight for liberty reached its peak, in the person of the Baptist missionary, William Knibb.

The story touches on natural disasters, dangerous social unrest, and trivia, such as the largest June fish haul, and the biggest yam and pumpkin produced in the parish.

There are glimpses of the rowdy life of Falmouth and of grand social occasions, highlighted by the annual Trelawny races and the glittering balls at the imposing Court House.

In Trelawny, perhaps more than in any other parish, there was a notion of "gentry," to which all who had the means sought to aspire. However, the arch conservatives were counter-balanced by a pugnacious, crusading newspaper editor, who repeatedly stormed their citadels.

The story contains dashes of humour, mystery, drama, and tragedy. It ends with Falmouth's decline in the late 1920s, symbolized by the fire which almost destroyed the magnificent Court House.

# THE BIRTH OF TRELAWNY AND FALMOUTH

The year 1655 was a tough one in Jamaica. It was the final year of the Spanish colony; the year of the English invasion.

The Spanish governor surrendered to the English, but a Resistance force, including a group of African servitors, held out for five years. Except for the Africans, the Resistance force was driven out in 1660, and the hard-pressed English were able to establish Civil government.

They started large-scale sugar production in 1664, and began dividing the island into parishes. A big parish was set up in the underpopulated North side in 1665. It was called St. James, in honour of his Royal Highness, James, Duke of York, brother of Charles II, the reigning monarch. James would succeed Charles as King in 1684.

St. James included the area now known as *Trelawny*. In 1673, the English settlers in the parish were estimated at only 89 men, 20 women and 15 children. With them were 22 Africans.

Two men were elected to represent St. James in the House of Assembly in 1675. The parish had few plantations, no towns and very little commerce. Up to 1693, it paid less taxes than any other parish; and in 1707, it had only one Justice of the Peace.

The introduction of large-scale sugar production in 1664 brought an increasing demand for labour. Captive Africans were brought in to provide the work force. The most spirited escaped into the mountains and forests and attacked settlers in parishes such as St. James and St. George (now part of Portland). Despite all efforts, they could not be eliminated, and, after a while, the English called them *Maroons*.

In 1730, an Act was approved for "the better suppressing and reducing" of rebellious and runaway slaves. Commissioners were appointed to raise a War Party in Hanover and St. James: "to range the woods from the west end of the island through the mountains, Little River and Negro River, Spanish Quarters and Martha Brae, to the westernmost boundaries of St. Ann."

A maroon village called Wiles Town was captured in 1732. It stood twenty-eight miles from Montego Bay (between Falmouth and Duncans) and near Mountain Spring. Maroon activities increased and some settlers were forced to leave the parish. Several took refuge in the neighbouring parish of St. Ann.

The first law for constructing a proper parish road was passed in 1724. The bad roads made it very difficult to attend court in Spanish Town, the then capital of Jamaica. The settlers sent a petition to the House of Assembly asking that an Assize Court for the County of Cornwall (in which St. James lay) be held at Montego Bay and Savanna-la-Mar.

The St. James settlers also complained that their parish was too large. Some had a hard time getting to the parish capital (Montego Bay) to transact business. They wrote the Assembly asking that the parish be divided.

In April 1733, the Assembly informed the Governor (Major-General Robert Hunter) that they had divided it. They asked him to give the new parish a name. The Governor suggested the name "Brunswick," probably because George II, the reigning monarch, was descended from the German Elector of *Brunswick-Luneburg*, also known as *Hanover*. However, thirty-seven years would pass before the new parish was actually formed.

The British finally made peace with the Maroons in 1739. At that time, there were only eight sugar estates in St. James, making together six hundred and sixty hogheads of sugar. Four of these estates belonged to a family called Lawrence.

Once the Maroon menace was removed, St. James began to develop. From only eight sugar estates in 1739, dozens and dozens more were soon established; and a new generation of citizens renewed the request for St. James to be divided.

In 1771, the Government published a "formal writ", declaring the division of St. James. The new parish was called, not Brunswick, as had been proposed, but Trelawny, in honour of the then Governor, William Trelawny. He came from a family rooted in the county of Cornwall in Britain, and was the second member of his family to serve as Governor of Jamaica. The first was *Edward Trelawny*, who had made peace with the Maroons in 1739.

At first, the chief town of Trelawny was Martha Brae. Near Martha Brae was a little seaside village known as Martha Brae Point, which was renamed Falmouth, after Governor Trelawny's birthplace. Around 1790, Falmouth took the place of Martha Brae as the capital of Trelawny. It had a little over two hundred houses at the time.

The town was built on flat land, just about level with the sea, which formed its northern border. The other three sides were bordered by swamps. The new capital experienced a "boom" in its early years and it was not unusual to see nearly thirty ships in Falmouth harbour, unloading cargo and taking on sugar, rum, etc. It took about six men to roll one hogshead of sugar onto the wharf, and additional hands were needed to hoist the hogsheads and store them aboard ship. So the port activities generated considerable employment.

Ships remained in port for four weeks or longer, depending on the weather. Sailors swarmed into town and spent money lavishly. Overseers and bookkeepers from sugar estates rode in, when their duties allowed, to join the lively scene. Things got so lively that in 1794, the Vestry (the Local Government body) passed a resolution that:-

> *All sailors found in grog shops or loitering about the streets of Falmouth, Martha Brae to the Rock, after the hour of six in the evening, be taken up by the Constable and put in confinement until morning, when they shall be arraigned before a magistrate, to be dealt with as directed by the law.*

In 1803, the authorities were forced to construct a "Cage" in the town square, in which to lock up drunken and disorderly sailors.

# TRELAWNY'S MAROON WAR

After about 56 years of relative peace, two Maroons from Trelawny Town were arrested in Montego Bay, in 1795, for stealing pigs. Trelawny Town was in St. James, and was one of the semi-independent communities recognized by the Maroon Peace Treaties of 1739. It was named after Governor Edward Trelawny, and was the "home-base" of Cudjoe, the paramount Maroon leader in the pre-treaty days.

The two accused pig thieves from Trelawny Town were tried and sentenced to be whipped at the tail of a cart. The authorities made the mistake of carrying out the punishment in the common workhouse in the presence of slaves. What was even worse, the whipping was done by a runaway slave who had been captured by Maroons. One of the terms of the 1739 Peace Treaties required the Maroons to help the Colonial government to defend the island, and to capture and return runaway slaves.

To the proud Trelawny Maroons, the punishment-whip, wielded by a slave, was the gravest imaginable insult. The news spread rapidly, and as the two "pig stealers" made their way home, they were mocked in the streets of Montego Bay, and laughed at on every plantation through which they passed. It made no difference that they were held in little regard by their own people. The manner of their punishment was still felt to be a severe blow to the prestige of the Trelawny Maroons. They had been humiliated; ridiculed and laughed at by slaves.

The young men of Trelawny Town were furious. They were the grandsons and great-grandsons of the warriors who had fought under Cudjoe, and won the peace in 1739. While they possessed the confidence and fighting spirit of their grandfathers and great-grandfathers, they were different in significant ways. They had become arrogant basking in the noble achievements of their ancestors, but without the maturity of outlook that their ancestors had been forced to develop, during their long, hard and painful struggle. They were rather like the spoilt sons of famous fathers.

The angry young men decided to strike out against the disgrace which the two worthless fellows had brought upon the whole community. John Tharpe, the Custos of Trelawny, led a deputation to Trelawny Town in an effort to mollify the Maroons, but the majority was determined to fight, to somehow wipe out the stain on their honour.

The war lasted for about seven months. Twenty actions were fought during that terrific struggle in the rugged Cockpit country, as a force of nearly five thousand (Regular troops, Militia, Accompong Maroons, Mosquito[1] Indians and savage Cuban hunting dogs) strove mightily to overcome about two hundred and fifty Trelawny Town Maroons, and some fugitive slaves. Among the many casualties were three senior British officers: Colonels Sandford, Gallimore and Fitch.

The Trelawny Regiment of Foot and the Trelawny Leeward Cavalry Troop were involved in one of the earliest, (and perhaps the most dramatic) encounters. They were among the contingent under Colonel William Sandford, which was caught in an ambush on a narrow trail between the Old Town and the New Town of the Trelawny Maroons. The Regiment of Foot was only saved from the death trap because it had been unable to keep pace with the Cavalry's rapid advance. When the Maroons opened fire, the Foot

---

[1] Also Mesquitto/ Mosquitto

Regiment retreated to the New Town from which the march had started. They remained there all night, thus saving themselves from casualties. Thirty-seven men died in the ambush, including Colonel Sandford. The war finally ended in February, 1796, when the Trelawny Maroons agreed to lay down their arms, on the understanding that they would not be exiled. Shortly after, however, they were shipped away, first to Nova Scotia in Canada, and later to Sierra Leone in Africa.

Peace did not last for long. In 1798, runaway slaves, some of whom were survivors from the conflict with the Trelawny Maroons, launched a war against the outlying settlements. The rebellion flourished in the mountainous area which was now covered by provision grounds, as a result of a number of estates that had recently been established in the vicinity of the Cockpit country.

One of the rebel leaders was a man named Cuffee, who had run away on September 18, 1797, from his owner, James McGhie of Coxheath Pen. Cuffee set up camp in the vicinity of Windsor with a gang of forty-three. Among them were two other slaves of James McGhie; Polydore and March, who had escaped on October 12, 1795.

Also mentioned in the records was another rebel band of thirty, led by a young Congo man who had joined the Trelawny Maroons. When the Trelawny Maroons laid down their arms early in 1796, the Congo man had apparently remained at large. Cuffee, Polydore and March had a grudge against their owner, James McGhie, and the first place they attacked was Coxheath Pen, which belonged to McGhie.

On February 14, 1798, between nine and ten in the morning, they rushed from the woods armed with guns and cutlasses, and surprised Archer, a groom, who was at the stables with the horses. Archer had two fierce Spanish dogs with him. He set them on the three advancing men, then ran off to neighbouring Windsor Pen, where his overseer, John Young, had gone on a visit.

Cuffee, Polydore and March fought off the dogs. A blow from a cutlass severed half an ear of one dog, and the other was killed inside the house. The three men plundered the house and returned to the woods. John Young, the overseer of Coxheath Pen, having been alerted by Archer the groom, hurried home, accompanied by the Windsor Pen overseer and carpenter, McNeish and Brown. By the time they arrived, the rebels had vanished.

On April 2, Cuffee and about six of his men broke into the house of a settler named Navin. It was nearing midnight. Navin was in bed, apparently with his housekeeper, Mary Clapham, a "free woman of colour". Cuffee demanded gunpowder and threatened to cut off Navin's head with the large sword he was carrying; but Mary held on to the sword and begged for her employer's life.

The rebels took away two hundred musket balls, a gun, a pistol, clothes, liquor, and other items. They went on to the Red Hill House owned by Robert Dixon, which stood near a place known as the *Lagoon*. They plundered and burnt the house, and also set fire to the house of Shacklock, a "free man of colour".

That same month, the second driver on Peru Estate, who was called Boatswain, persuaded several newly-arrived Mandingoes and Coromantees to run off with him and join the rebels. Boatswain returned to Peru that night and was captured. He was put into the stocks with three other slaves, prior to being taken to Falmouth. His followers broke into the room where he was being held, burnt the woodwork of the stocks, tore off the iron and freed him.

Six days later, two settlers, Henry Paulett and Alexander Steel, were sitting on the piazza of a house in Ventura Settlement with two acquaintances, Joseph Biggs and Thomas Kew. At about 4 p.m., a quadroon woman named Rebecca Pleasure Wilton, ran up and told them the place was surrounded by rebels. They jumped up and got their guns. Steel and Kew took up positions on either side of the back door. Paulett and Biggs stationed themselves at a window in one of the rooms.

Shots rang out. A bullet went through Kew's head, killing him on the spot. Another bullet grazed Paulett, "raising the skin on his chest" and a third passed through Biggs' right shoulder.

Just then, Billy, a loyal slave, ran into the house, picked up the gun which Kew had dropped, and began shooting at the attackers. Steel, Paulett, Biggs, and Billy held off the rebels for hours. Five times the rebels tried to set the house on fire, but each time Billy helped to put out the flames at the risk of his life. The rebels called him a "damn Chambo, cut-faced son-of-a-bitch".

Over at neighbouring Gray's Inn Settlement, Thomas Johnson heard the shots coming from Ventura. He armed a group of faithful slaves and went to see what was happening; but he couldn't get through the ring of rebels. He returned to Gray's Inn and kept guard all night.

At sunrise, some of Paulett's slaves approached the Ventura house. The rebels fired and drove them off, then set fire to the storehouse containing one thousand two hundred pounds of cured coffee, three thousand pounds of yam, carpenter's tools, and other supplies. Everything was consumed.

From Gray's Inn, Thomas Johnson could see smoke rising from Ventura. A little later, rebels went past his house. They called out saying they would be returning to eat *Second Breakfast*, with him. In Jamaica, in the old days, a meal called Second Breakfast was served at about one in the afternoon. It was the equivalent to today's lunch.

Thomas Johnson decided not to wait for that threatened visit for Second Breakfast. He collected the weapons with which he had armed his faithful slaves, abandoned the Gray's Inn house and fled to Coxheath Pen.

Steel and Paulett, waiting tensely in the Ventura house, thought that things seemed fairly quiet outside. They opened a window. When no shots were fired they threw all their valuables on the piazza for their slaves to carry and hurried through the woods to Duan Vale Estate.

On the same day (April 18), John White and Humphrey Colquhoun reported from Black River in St. Elizabeth that fifty or sixty rebels had come out of the woods, destroyed a mountain settlement and killed the overseer (a free man of colour). It wasn't clear whether the St. Elizabeth group was connected to the Trelawny rebels.

Alarmed by these events, the Custos of Trelawny, James Irving, wrote the governor, the Earl of Balcarres. He asked for permission to instruct Colonel Robert Bell of the Trelawny Militia to fit out parties to go after the rebels. He also requested reinforcements of regular troops from the 84th Regiment. The governor gave permission, but Colonel Bell had a hard time finding recruits; according to him: "everyone wishes to put the burden on his neighbour's shoulders".

The force which Bell eventually assembled consisted of settlers who had experience of fighting in the woods, "free coloureds and confidential slaves, some of whom had served as Black Shots in the Maroon War".

Trelawny had not yet recovered from the effects of the Maroon War. Many back settlements had been abandoned. Now, with the new outbreak, families in the vicinity of the danger zone were moving to safer places. Among those leaving were: Reid and Brisbane, McDorman, McKane, Flemming, Navin, Wills, Houghstead, Patterson, and Alexander Elgan. Also clearing out were Shacklock and Dickson who were carpenters; Mrs. Graves, a widow with several children; Mrs. Watt and family, and Steel and Paulett.

On May 15, William Green reported from Good Hope Estate that rebels had driven the slaves out of the grounds of Pantrepant, and set fire to a house adjoining the property. The rebels said they would be going to the Reid and Brisbane Settlement, about a mile beyond Pantrepant. If the soldiers and militia wanted to seek them there, they

---

[2] The *Black Shots* were contingents of "trusted" slaves who were trained and armed to help in the fight against Maroons and rebels.

would give them "a belly-full of fighting". Soldiers and militia hurried to Pantrepant and put out the fire; William Green felt that if the rebellion was not checked soon, "it would turn into a second Santo Domingo (Haiti) war, as disaffected slaves were daily joining the rebels".

On the same day as the incident at Pantrepant, George Brissett reported from Mahogany Hall that Knowle's Settlement in the Black Grounds had been burnt. Slaves from the settlement were threatening to attack Mahogany Hall and Sportsman's Hall.

A slave from Peru Estate named Peter, who volunteered to serve under Colonel Bell as a Black Shot, was captured by Cuffee and Polydore, along with a Creole boy and "an Eboe wench". After a trial in the woods, Peter was sentenced to death. His clothes were stripped off. Cuffee slashed at Peter with his cutlass; but Peter warded off the blow. Cuffee lost his balance and fell. Peter sprang into the bushes and ran. Cuffee's two companions snapped their guns at him; but good luck was with Peter and both guns misfired.

The rebels pursued. Peter, running with the speed of desperation, out-distanced his heavily-armed pursuers. He lost sight of them. When he came to the top of a hill, he climbed a tall, leafy tree and stayed there all day. At about eight o'clock on the morning of May 23, he emerged from the woods at Windsor Pen, safe and sound.

Peter informed the authorities that the rebels planned to burn Fontabelle, Peru and all the black settlements in that part of the country. They intended to "drive all the people before them" to "get room to burn Hampstead (and) kill James McGhie". Peter reported that he heard Cuffee and Polydore say that once they got their old master, James McGhie, "they would be done".

The man who was largely responsible for finally breaking up the rebellion was Captain Lauchlan McLain of the St. James Black Shots. McLain had served in the Trelawny Maroon War as commander of the same Black Shot Company he was now leading. He had personally disciplined and inspired the company which had taken part in three successive actions against the dreaded Trelawny Maroons.

On the night of June 5, Lauchlan McLain, marched with the St. James Black Shots from Caledonia to Reid and Brisbane, hoping to take Cuffee by surprise; he saw a light in the house of a man named Rattray. Suspecting that rebels were in the house, he left part of his men "under the hill" and began moving stealthily around the house with the rest. But a nervous raw recruit mistook a Black Shot named Cato for a rebel, and shot him dead. The shot alerted Cuffee. A horn was blown and a drum beaten. Cuffee shouted in the darkness, challenging him to wait until the moon rose before launching his attack.

McLain waited; but when the moon rose, Cuffee and his men were nowhere to be seen. To make matters worse, the moonlight revealed that five Black Shots had deserted.

McLain joined forces with Captain Innes and his Trelawny Black Shots. On July 8, they came upon what looked like the main rebel camp; a collection of huts called "the high Windward Town." Two of the foremost rebels, Prince and Hercules, were slain; and three women were captured. The hero of the fight was Sergeant James Hall of the Trelawny Black Shots. Major General McMurdo of the Militia recommended Hall for a reward, saying that he had gone out with every party of the Trelawny company that entered the woods, and had done essential service "in discovering and tracking the intricate paths of the rebels". Whenever the party was approaching the rebels, Hall always requested that he be put in command of the advanced guard, "and always acquitted himself with spirit and good conduct".

What eventually happened to the rebel leaders, Polydore and March, is not clear; but after the capture of the High Windward Town, the war petered out.

The 1795 Trelawny Maroon War had so shaken the authorities that they had taken no chances in the conflict with the rebels. They had sent in 2,000 Regular Troops,

6,000 Militia and a contingent of Accompong Maroons to subdue what turned out to be two or three determined rebel gangs.

# FALMOUTH GROWS AND PROSPERS

In spite of the desperate struggles with Maroons and rebels, Trelawny continued to prosper. Drogher boats (coasting vessels) traded between Falmouth, St. Ann's Bay, Dry Harbour, Rio Bueno and Montego Bay, with lumber and imported provisions. Fish and lumber came in on schooners from Halifax in Canada. Vessels arrived from England loaded with coal, flour, biscuits, liquor and dry goods of all sorts. Mule carts brought pimento, coffee, annatto and other goods from farms in the interior of Trelawny. Falmouth was a focus of activity, and on public holidays, soldiers had to assist the regular police to keep order.

The Falmouth Parish Church was built at a cost of ten thousand pounds, and completed in 1795. The site consisted of four lots of land donated by one of Trelawny's leading citizens, the Hon. Edward Barrett. The organ was presented by John Tharpe Esq, who belonged to one of the parish's most powerful planting families.

On November 7, 1798, a petition of the merchants, traders and other inhabitants of Trelawny was presented to the House of Assembly, saying that, for a considerable time, a great number of transient traders had been coming to Falmouth:-

> *Where they have been enabled to dispose of their goods and merchandise on lower terms than the resident traders could do, who are subject to public and parochial taxes, store rent and other expenses and charges.*

## FALMOUTH GROWS AND PROSPERS

The petitioners asked that a law be passed to assess a transient tax in the parish. In 1800, the public taxes paid by the free people of Trelawny amounted to twenty thousand seven hundred and fifty-five pounds and ten pence.

> *"13,295 hogshead, 1,229 tierces of sugar, 6,400 Puncheons of Rum, besides other produce" were shipped at the wharves of Falmouth and the Rock, a thriving little village with several wharves. In that year, Trelawny had "one hundred sugar estates, 128 Penns and other settlements".*
>
> *Taxes were paid on 27,636 slaves, 17,619 heads of stock and 256 carriage wheels. For years, the parish had more slaves than any other parish in Jamaica.*

Originally, the town got its water from the Martha Brae River, a mile away; but in 1797 and 1798, some citizens organized a company and got a charter to supply water to the town and to ships lying in the harbour. Operations started at Martha Brae with a diversion canal, dam, aqueduct, sluice gate and a twenty-foot Persian wheel. The wheel dropped water into a wooden trough, the water ran into a six-inch main, and then on into the square at Falmouth, where it was stored in a reservoir. The square became known as Water Square.

On January 11, 1801, twenty thousand pounds was subscribed in one hour to finance the water scheme. The Falmouth Water Company (a Corporate body constituted under an Act of the Legislature), was given the power to tax those who benefited from the piped water supply. Equipment for the water system was shipped from England.

From being an insignificant village in 1780, Falmouth, between 1800 and 1802, could now be classed among the largest towns in the island. A great deal of business was being transacted, but some inhabitants felt that much more could be done if the town was made a Port of Entry. The harbour was defended by a reef, and was spacious, safe, and capable of much improvement. The channel leading into it ran "about North-East and South-East," making it very secure against the strong north winds which prevailed in the winter months. One hundred square-rigged vessels and fifth-one schooners and sloops, anchored and sailed from the harbour during the twelve months of the year 1802.

**The Water Wheel**

# THE BARRETTS & THARPES

Two of the wealthiest plantation-owning families in Trelawny were the Barretts and the Tharpes. The first Barrett is said to have come to Jamaica with the English force, under Penn and Venables, which, in 1655, captured the island from Spain. His name was Hearcey Barrett. In 1660 when the army was disbanded, Hearcey Barrett settled at Withywood, now known as Vere.

The Barretts were given a huge tract of land on the north side of the island (a deed of gift from King Charles II), and Hearcey's grandson, Samuel, was the first of the family to settle there, in about 1715.

Samuel Barrett had a son named Edward, born in 1734. When Samuel died, Edward was twenty-four, and Samuel left his estates to him. The sugar industry was now at its peak, and great fortunes were being made by large plantation owners. Young Edward was able to lay his hands on plenty of money to modernize and develop his estates. At the sugar works at Cinnamon Hill, (which was one of his estates) an aqueduct on massive stone pillars, thirty-feet high, is one of the surviving monuments to the work of Edward Barrett.

Apart from their land grant, the Barretts acquired other properties, and their holdings on the north side were said to have stretched from Cinnamon Hill in St. James all along the seacoast towards the eastern border of Trelawny: "from the Little River to Falmouth."

It is not surprising, therefore, that the Barretts were associated with THE BIRTH OF FALMOUTH in a very practical way. Shortly after Trelawny became a parish, Edward Barrett drew up a plan for a town to be built on one of his properties called 'Palmetto Point'. It lay on the seacoast, north of Martha Brae, which had become the chief town of Trelawny. Martha Brae was about a mile upstream from the mouth of the Martha Brae River. There was a place with wharves at the Rock near the river's mouth, but it was shallow. It was soon obvious that a seacoast parish like Trelawny would be better served by a town with a seaport of adequate depth; so the authorities turned to Barrett's proposed town site which was a little further along the coast. It was described, in 1774, as being "a proper place for the erection of a town, situated very conveniently for carrying on trade and merchandise. For that purpose, the said Edward Barrett hath laid out and planned a town called... Barrett Town, regularly divided into streets and lots." In 1775, he sold lots to Samuel Reeves and John Sylvester, "two free mulattoes who were carpenters." In 1778, he sold a waterfront lot to John Tharpe.

Falmouth developed out of Barrett Town, and when a parish church was to be built, the Barretts donated land for the purpose.

The wealth of the Barretts, of course, was built on the back of slave labour, but that was the way business was done on the plantations and in the mines of the Americas and the Caribbean in those days. It was all legal and supported by the established church, and rich West Indian planters were welcome in the highest social circles. The Barretts were said to have treated their slaves well and were rewarded with faithful service and loyalty. A Barrett slave jumped in front of his master during the Trelawny Maroon War, and took a bullet intended for his master (George Goodin Barrett). The slave fortunately recovered. On the day following the outbreak of the Sam Sharpe Rebellion (December, 1831) when several estates around were in ashes and their slaves were in arms, the Barrett slaves on Cinnamon Hill and Cornwall turned out for work as usual.

Kindness not withstanding, business was business, and a member of the Barrett family, the Hon. Richard Barrett of Barrett Hall and Greenwood (Speaker of the Jamaican House of Assembly) worked diligently against the abolition of slavery, as did just about everybody who benefited from the institution. He was twice sent to England by his colleagues, to argue the case of the Jamaican slave owners. But there was already emerging another member of the Barrett family, perhaps the most famous, who would give thanks for the abolition of slavery.

Edward Moulton Barrett of Cinnamon Hill (the Builder) had three children, two boys and a girl. The girl, Elizabeth, married Charles Moulton and had several children. The eldest of these was also named Edward, and he became the heir of old Edward the Builder, his grandfather. He left Jamaica as a boy, and apparently never returned. When his grandfather, old Edward, died, and he became heir to the Jamaican properties in 1798, he and his brother Samuel took the additional surname of Barrett. Up to that time, their name was Moulton. Now they were Moulton Barrett. It probably had something to do with the conditions of the inheritance, that the name Barrett should continue to be associated with the Jamaican properties.

In 1805, at the age of twenty, Edward Moulton Barrett (as he now was) got married. He left his Jamaican estates to be looked after by his brother Samuel, who lived in the island from time to time. Edward Moulton Barrett had eleven children who survived. The eldest was a girl, born in 1806 and christened Elizabeth. She was to become the famous English poet, Elizabeth Barrett Browning, wife of the poet, Robert Browning.

Edward Moulton Barrett became one of the most eccentric, patriarchal figures in the society of his time. He refused to give permission for his children to become romantically involved with anyone or to get married. They lived in a mansion on Wimpole Street and he was determined to keep them at home and under his control.

In 1833, when the bill to abolish slavery was being debated in the British Parliament, Edward Moulton Barrett said that if the bill was passed, nobody in their senses would think of even attempting to grow sugar, and they might as well hang weights on Jamaica and sink it at once. Edward Moulton Barrett was the owner of Cinnamon Hill and Cornwall, and half a dozen other estates in Jamaica, which he had never bothered to visit. When slavery was abolished on August 1, 1834, the British government gave compensation to slave owners for the loss of their human property. Edward Moulton Barrett expected to get 140,000 pounds, but he only got 20,000. He was a very bitter man, for he had over 2,000 slaves. His daughter Elizabeth (the poet) said:"The bill has ruined the West Indians (the Plantation owners). That is settled. The consternation here is very great. Nevertheless, I am glad, and always shall be that the (people) are virtually free."

In December 1846, she wrote a friend to say that she was sending an anti-slavery poem to America, but she didn't think it would be published because it was "too ferocious". In 1853, she wrote another letter praising Harriet Beecher Stowe's anti-slavery novel *Uncle Tom's Cabin*. She said she honoured America, but "would not be an American for the world while she wears the shameful scar (of slavery) upon her brow." Slavery was not abolished in America until 1863. "I belong to a family of West Indian slaveholders," she said, "and if I believed in curses, I should be afraid."

Slavery and oppression were as old as human cultures and societies. At the time of Elizabeth Barrett's birth, most people still lived under the rule of oppressors. It was not surprising that some slaves, especially when born into the slave system, should be grateful for kind masters and be willing to die for them. In the Americas and the Caribbean, slavery became an ethnic and racial thing, targeting Africans and people of African descent, and having dreadful consequences long after slavery itself was abolished. Elizabeth Barrett understood this.

In 1844, Elizabeth Barrett met the poet Robert Browning. In the early months of 1845, they began writing to each other, being forced to keep their growing relationship secret, because of old Edward Moulton Barrett's attitude. In March, 1846, the lovers became secretly engaged. In September, they were married and hurried off to France.

Edward Moulton Barrett never forgave his daughter, or opened any of her letters to him. Elizabeth and Robert Browning lived a happily married life for fifteen years: "Happy as two owls in a hole; two toads under a tree stump." Elizabeth died in 1861.

Robert Browning wrote nearly three hundred poems, and devoted his life exclusively to poetry. He was ranked with Tennyson as a major poet of the Victorian era. Elizabeth Barrett Browning was recognized during her lifetime as England's greatest woman poet. Apparently, she never used the name Moulton.

It is pleasing to think of Elizabeth Barrett Browning as the great granddaughter of Edward Barrett, who conceived the idea of laying out a seaport town which eventually grew into Falmouth, the capital of Trelawny; a place that was once known as BARRETT TOWN.

Like the Barretts, the Tharpes enjoyed the prestige associated with the ownership of extensive tracts of land.

Whereas Hearcey Barrett, the founder of the Barrett line in Jamaica, had come with the conquering English force, John Tharpe, who appears to have founded the Tharpe family in the island, didn't surface until nearly the middle of the 18th Century.

It was said that, in those days, when men were eager to grab as much real estate as they could, John Tharpe acquired enough land to enable him to ride from the sea near Martha Brae, over the Cockpit Country, and down to the sea on the south, without ever leaving his property. Allowing for some exaggeration, and considering the size of Jamaica, that was a tremendous hunk of property, fit for a principality or dukedom.

The words of Alexander Selkirk, describing the circumstances of Robinson Crusoe, the castaway, might well be applied to John Tharpe at the peak of his fortune:-

> *"I am monarch of all I survey,*
> *My right there is none to dispute.*
> *From the centre all round to the sea,*
> *I am lord of the fowl and the brute."*

**A building on Good Hope Estate**

John Tharpe was a self-made man, not very unusual in the raw, frontier days of the Americas and the Caribbean. In the pages of plantation history, he first draws attention as the overseer of Good Hope Estate, one of the most famous establishments in Trelawny. Good Hope became famous for the beauty of its buildings and its splendid hospitality. The sugar industry was approaching its peak, and the lifestyle in plantation homes with resident families, was lavish. There was little in the way of public entertainment for country dwellers, so entertainment had to be generated within the estates. Friends and relatives would usually visit for weeks. There was lots of food and drink, armies of servants; singing, dancing, horseback riding, games and general merrymaking. Good Hope was in the forefront of this lavish lifestyle.

Good Hope appeared to have been established in about 1744, by Colonel Thomas Williams. He was succeeded as the owner by his son Obediah. John Tharpe was Obediah's overseer. Like many other successful (and not-so-successful) planters, Obediah became an absentee landholder, leaving his plantation to be run by others. This was a very dangerous practice as the plantation managerial class, which kept the estates running for the absentee owners were often concerned primarily with filling their own pockets at the expense of their employers. Before long, Good Hope began to run down, and after awhile it passed into the hands of John Tharpe.

Allan Furness, a graduate of Cambridge University, claimed that he researched the Tharpe family history from over two thousand business and private letters, legal papers and account books of the estates found at Cambridge University, together with records in the Spanish Town Archives and extracts from the Falmouth Post newspaper. Furness said that John Tharpe came to Jamaica as a very young man (this was usually the case with many British fortune hunters at the time). His father and grandfather owned properties in Hanover. In 1766, he married the daughter of a Barbados planter who owned a property in Trelawny. From that point, John Tharpe's career as a landowner took off.

At the age of twenty-five, John Tharpe managed to buy Good Hope Estate on a sort of installment plan. He raised the money to purchase the land by selling the Hanover property of his deceased relatives, and borrowing from a planter named Miles. When Tharpe died, he still owed money to Miles.

Apart from Good Hope, Tharpe soon owned more estates than any other person in Trelawny. His estates included Covey, Lansquinet, Merrywood, Pantrepant, Potosi, Top Hill, Wales and Windsor. It will also be remembered that in 1778, he bought a waterfront lot in Barrett Town from Edward Barrett.

John Tharpe returned to England in 1791, and bought an estate in Newmarket and a town house in London. He returned to Jamaica soon after, and, in 1795, when the Trelawny Maroons were threatening to go to war, he was the Custos and Chief Magistrate of Trelawny. With the agreement of the leading Maroons, he led a deputation to Trelawny Maroon Town for a peace conference. The deputation promised to bring the grievances of the Maroons before the House of Assembly. However, rumours spread that the Maroons, encouraged by Haitian rebel slaves, were determined to fight, and the work of Tharpe's deputation was undone when fighting broke out.

Tharpe, like the Barretts, had his own wharf and offices in Falmouth. Many years after the Tharpe "empire" had passed away, the Tharpe shipping complex in Falmouth would become the government's Collectorate and Customs House with its pier. Tharpe also had a town house and residences on Market and George streets in Falmouth, but Good Hope was the centre of activity, a gathering place for many of the Plantocrats of the parish.

Most prosperous and well-run estates were like little villages. They usually had a big house with offices for the owner or manager, a mill, a boiling house, large curing houses, a still house, roomy stables for the cattle which turned the mill, quarters for the overseer and European servants, working shops for the smiths, carpenters and coopers, and rows of houses for the slaves. Good Hope had all this and more, including a hospital and resident physician, a foundry, a church and a burial ground. The,

"Gentry" of the parish met at Good Hope in an atmosphere of conviviality, to discuss all aspects of the sugar economy. Even the Governor of Jamaica was motivated to go to Good Hope. In April, 1802, the then Governor-General George Nugent, accompanied by his wife, Lady Nugent, who wrote the famous "Journal," were the guests of Mr. Tharpe at Good Hope. Lady Nugent wrote that Mr. Tharpe of Good Hope, Trelawny, came next to Mr. Simon Taylor of St. Thomas in respectability, and as the owner of extensive properties in Jamaica.

Tharpe had over two thousand slaves. Like the Barretts it was said that the Tharpes treated their slaves with great consideration.

In the midst of the apparent success of his enterprises, Tharpe's second son and heir, Joseph, died. He returned to England where he greatly improved his estate, and undertook work to upgrade boiling equipment in order to make his plantations more profitable. He also arranged for his grandson, also named John, and who was little more than an infant, to become his heir.

Tharpe's wife died and he married again; but his second wife was seduced by his daughter's husband, who was a clergyman. Tharpe hurried back to Jamaica in 1802. He was sick, unhappy, suffering from gout; still mourning for his dead son, Joseph. That was the year Governor-General Nugent and his wife visited Good Hope. As if trying to overcome his sorrows, Tharpe now began to spend a lot of money planting a new variety of cane that had been developed in the West Indies. He died soon after, in 1804.

According to Allan Furness, Tharpe's grandson, John, who was only ten years old when Tharpe died, began to develop into a lunatic. The estates left to him by his grandfather were controlled by executors until he was twenty-four. In Tharpe's will, six hundred tons of sugar were granted annually to pay off the debt still owing to Miles who had lent Tharpe money to help finance his purchase of lands. Grandson John was manoeuvred into marrying into an aristocratic English family (no doubt for his West Indian assets), and this apparently drove him completely insane. He was put into a private asylum where he lived to be almost ninety, much to the distress of relatives who would have liked to get their hands on his property. His uncle tried to get hold of the estates and the battle raged for many years. In 1829, there were 2,583 slaves on nine Tharpe properties.

The Tharpe sugar empire in Jamaica, like every other slave owning establishment large and small, was hit hard by Britain's abolition of slavery throughout its empire, and by full Emancipation in Jamaica in 1838. The Tharpe enterprises, like others, began to crumble. Some said that bad management and inattention had already started the process of decay; and that the Tharpes were too lax with their slaves, too generous. According to Allan Furness, another of Tharpe's grandsons, William (descended by what route is not quite clear), displayed the same concern for the slaves as John Tharpe by educating them and seeing about their spiritual needs. With the fall in the price of sugar, the estates became heavily indebted, but due to the technicalities of Tharpe's will, they could not be divided among the relatives.

Grandson John died in 1860, and the estates were sold at a loss, ending the Tharpe connection with Jamaica. In June, 1865, shortly before the Morant Bay Rebellion, the following Tharpe estates were sold: Good Hope, Covey, Lansquinet, Potosi, Pantrepant, Wales, Windsor Pen, Merrywood, Top Hill, Summer Hill Pens, Chippenham and Park Pen.

William Tharpe (John Tharpe's other grandson) appears quite frequently in the local history of Trelawny. He was a Captain in the Trelawny Militia Regiment at the time of the Sam Sharpe Rebellion; was one time owner of Windsor Castle and later owned Chester Castle. He died on November 18, 1847 at the age of forty-eight. A year after his death, his "second daughter," Eliza, who appeared to have some African ancestry, got married to a "quadroon" gentleman named John Reid, who was descended from a distinguished Trelawny planting family. The wedding took place on December 9, 1848, at the chapel on Good Hope Estate, which was owned by John, the insane grandson of John Tharpe. A daughter was born to John and Eliza Reid at Windsor Pen on March 15, 1850. She was christened Maria Tharpe Reid.

Many British planters, merchants, overseers, bookkeepers, craftsmen, etc in Jamaica had African mistresses or mistresses of some degree of African descent. Even some Governors with the highest-ranking titles of nobility had such mistresses. It was part of the way-of-life, and no lofty moral condemnation could shake it. The children of such unions were sometimes greatly cherished by their British fathers.

The dream of just about every British fortune hunter was to get rich as quickly as possible and return home to England, to live like a lord; and, if possible, to marry into the aristocracy or at least into the Gentry, if one did not already belong there. The Jamaican family unit, as represented by the mistress and her children, had no place in such a future.

The departing Plantocrats left their genes in many Jamaican families. The British who never made it back home likewise left their genes along with their names in thousands of Jamaican families. The DNA, as we now know, is virtually indestructible, despite outward appearances. Many descendants of the British in Jamaica would try to build on the foundations that some of their ancestors or taskmasters had found it expedient to abandon.

# THE SPLENDID GENTRY

Falmouth was tied to a number of sugar estates, Penns and other properties scattered in the country side of Trelawny beyond the town. Country properties were generally of four types:

**Sugar Estates:** where sugar, rum and molasses were produced;

**Plantations:** Where coffee, pimento, gingers, cotton, arrowroot and other minor crops were grown;

**Penns**: where horses, mules, steer and all kinds of livestock were bred, and from which butchers were supplied with cattle for the markets;

**Settlements**: on which grew logwood, fustic, lignum vitae, ebony, cedar, mahogany and also the food crops found on plantations.

The parish had a large and prosperous landed class, the cream of parish society, the ruling class, the SPLENDID GENTRY. How did such people live?

According to Bernard Senior ("Jamaica as it was, is and could be."), few of the better-off people lived in towns. Almost every merchant, medical or legal practitioner, etc, had a Penn (a comfortable and often handsome establishment) a short distance from town.

Very soon after daylight family members would mount their horses and ride for exercise until about seven or eight o'clock. If the family was religious, Morning Prayer would then be held and would be attended by any guest in the house.

Breakfast would be served at about nine. This would be a big meal which would include tea, coffee, chocolate (served personally by the ladies of the house), yams, (some crushed and mixed with milk and butter), roasted and boiled cocoa, roast plantains and sometimes potatoes, bread kind (hot rolls, toast, cascade cakes and sweet potatoes) a steak, chops or stew and in the centre of the table a cold ham or tongue. Other spaces on the table would be occupied by small dishes of "devilled" fowl or duck, boiled salt herring, broiled salmon, etc.

After breakfast, family members and any guests would go about the daily occupations and amusements, a ride around the property, a drive into town, a visit to neighbours perhaps to invite them to dinner, a shooting or fishing expedition. Women would do needle-work, read, play music or engage in numerous domestic concerns.

At one o'clock, the "second breakfast" would be served, consisting of fruits which were in season (pines, melons, mangoes, bananas, oranges, shaddocks, avocado pears, etc.), "tastefully mingled" with cold chicken, sliced ham, tongue, pickled salmon, cray fish, etc, along with bread kind, marmalade and preserves.

At about four o'clock the "dressing bell" would be rung and family members and guests would set aside whatever they were doing and begin to dress for dinner. While they were dressing, servants would sweep, and, if necessary, polish the wooden floors (often made of bullet tree wood and blood wood) using woolen cloths saturated with wax and moistened with Seville orange juice. When the company assembled for dinner they would be greeted with bright clean floors, often slippery with much shining.

A second ringing of the bell would announce the serving of the meal which would include a well-peppered soup (an essential part of the meal for many Jamaicans), fish, pastry and dessert accompanied by Madeira wine, Hock or Claret (Port and sherry were considered too heavy).

After dinner the ladies would leave the table to have coffee. The gentlemen would join them after awhile and the evening would then be filled with music and conversation. In those days of little public entertainment, and before the advent of radio and television, etc, households generated their own entertainment, and everyone was encouraged to participate. If the party was big enough there would be dancing.

At about ten the bell would ring again and everyone, including the servants, would unite in worship. A hymn was usually sung. Afterwards the ladies would retire. The men would drink a glass of weak spirits and water at the side-board before also going to bed. Sleepers were protected from mosquitoes by a muslin net usually attached to every bed. The peace and quiet of the country night would be deep and invariably unbroken by any jarring sounds.

The family had to live within itself. There were no nearby shops where articles could be purchased at any time. The nearest town was often twenty or thirty miles away and once a week the family would send there for letters and supplies. Otherwise the "fowl house", the kitchen garden, the fields and domestic livestock supplied food and milk. The ruined portion of the land yielded fuel for the family.

For transportation the family had either a phaeton or gig (or both if they were affluent), draft horses, riding horses and mules. Roads were usually so bad that when travelling to town or to visit neighbours the maximum speed would be about seven miles an hour. Anything faster might result in the springs of the vehicle being broken.

They streamed into Falmouth in their carriages or clattered in on horse back to attend significant occasions, such as a visit by a Governor, a grand ball or concert by visiting artiste, militia parades, horse racing etc. Some of them had town houses in Falmouth.

The citizens of Falmouth would gaze at them with great curiosity and sometimes critical eyes.

## THE 55TH AND THE FRENCH SCARE

In 1796, after the end of the Second Maroon War, a bill was tabled in the House of Assembly to appoint commissioners to sell the land of the Trelawny Maroons. The land had been granted to them fifty-seven years before, when they had signed the 1739 Peace Treaty. The bill proposed that a portion of the land should be reserved for troops who would be stationed at the site.

British troops in Jamaica had been dying at an alarming rate from diseases such as yellow fever. The excessive use of rum was a contributing factor, but there is no doubt that disease was the main killer. The troops lived mostly in "fever-ridden" camps. Even Up Park Camp, purchased in 1784, for the military, was found to be most unhealthy. Reports mentioned the garrison at Fort Augusta being twice swept away by fever.

Highland stations like the one at Stony Hill were found to be healthier; but it was not until 1841 that the healthiest military station of all was founded; 4,000 feet above sea-level in the Port Royal mountains. It was called Newcastle.

The military station in Maroon Town, situated in cool, hilly country, was expected to be a healthy place. Temporary barracks was built there, shortly after the Trelawny Maroons were exiled from Jamaica. Troops guarding Western Jamaica were quartered there, and also at the sea-port towns of Savanna-la-mar, Lucea, Montego Bay and Falmouth; and at the Black Grounds in Trelawny.

The original fort in Falmouth was built to one side of the town, near Water Square, where the Court House now stands. It was named Fort Balcarres, in honour of the Earl of

Balcarres, Governor of Jamaica from 1795 (when the second Maroon War began) to 1800. The town grew up around the fort, and the fort was soon surrounded by buildings.

The guns were often fired in ceremonial salutes, and the burning wads which flew from them, would drop on nearby roofs and sometimes set them on fire. It became uncomfortable to live with the fort where it was, so, in about 1802, it was moved from the centre of the town nearer to the sea. At around that time, it was garrisoned by a detachment of the 83rd Regiment of Foot, which had fought vigorously in the second Maroon War, and whose commander (Colonel William Fitch) had been killed in an ambush.

On May 26, 1802, while General George Nugent (husband of Lady Nugent, author of the famous "Journal") was governor, two warships, Alkmaar and Druid, arrived at Port Royal with the 55th Regiment of Foot, which had recently been serving in Europe. The 55th was to relieve detachments of the 83rd Regiment at Savanna-la-mar, Lucea, Montego Bay and Falmouth, and also the Second Battalion of the 85th Regiment at Maroon Town.

The Alkmaar arrived at Montego Bay on Friday, 28 May. The next day was the anniversary of the restoration of Charles II.

A Royal salute was fired from the fort and, in the afternoon, the men of the 55th went ashore. A detachment under Major Godfrey McDonald marched to the barracks and relieved the soldiers of the 83rd, who boarded the Alkmaar. The next morning, Major Halkett marched with the remainder of the 55th to Maroon Town, where they relieved the Second Battalion of the 85th, under Lieutenant Colonel Lord Aylmer, which marched to Montego Bay and embarked on the Alkmaar.

The Druid meanwhile had dropped detachments of the 55th at Savanna-la-mar and Lucea, and taken on the men of the 85th. She reached Falmouth on Thursday, June 3, and dropped off the remainder of the 55th under Captain Dickson, which marched to Fort Balcarres. The detachment of the 83rd, which they relieved, embarked on the Druid. Alkmaar and Druid then returned to Port Royal with the men of the 83rd and the 85th.

On Monday, June 28, the 83rd and the 69th regiments marched from Spanish Town to Port Henderson. They were to sail from there to England, along with the 20th Light Dragoons; but most of the 83rd and 69th wanted to remain in Jamaica.

The 83rd had certainly been in the island for many years. Some of them had apparently put down roots, and acquired loved ones they didn't want to leave. So they volunteered to serve in regiments that were in the island. There were always gaps to be filled, because of the high death rate, so the authorities welcomed the volunteers. Each man received a bounty of three guineas. In July 1802, some of these volunteers arrived at Montego Bay on HMS Ceres, to join the 55th, which had already begun to lose men.

Captain Dixon, in charge of the detachment stationed at Martha Brae, was paid fifty-four pounds, ten shillings "towards defraying the expense of burying thirty-four soldiers and three soldiers' wives". They died between June 12 and December 6, 1802.

Up in the healthier atmosphere of Maroon Town, Archibald Guthrie, surgeon of the 55th, and Henry Kearns, the quarter-master, died in October, and in Savanna-la-mar Lieutenant William Dickson died in November.

Philip Barrington Ainslie, a Scottish youth of seventeen, came to Falmouth shortly before the arrival of the 55th, although he got his dates wrong in writing his memoirs many years later. He had come to take up a job as book-keeper on a sugar estate. Ainslie described the large detachment of the 55th quartered at Falmouth as: "mostly fine, strong, hearty men (whose) ruddy cheeks and healthy looks appeared in strong contrast with the pale, wan complexions and listless gait" of the white creole inhabitants. He thought this was due to the effects of the climate on the long-time residents.

While in Falmouth, Ainslie stayed with Mr. Baillie, the Civilian Commandant of Fort Balcarres. Baillie's house stood just behind the fort, which overlooked the harbour. Every morning, Ainslie watched from the house as the soldiers of the 55$^{th}$ were marched to the beach, where they stripped, plunged into the sea and swam about. A line of boats rowed up and down outside the area where they bathed to protect them from shards.

General George Nugent, the new governor, made an official visit to Falmouth soon after Ainslie's arrival. Mr. Baillie ordered a salute to be fired from the fort, and his unmarried sister, who looked after his "large, handsome" house, was greatly alarmed. She feared that the noise of the guns would shatter the glass windows, several of which were glazed, a very unusual feature at that time.

Governor Nugent landed with Admiral John Duckworth, commander of the fleet on the Jamaica station. The Governor was immediately taken to review the Infantry and Light Dragoons of the Trelawny Militia Regiment. There was a large gathering of spectators, of all classes and colours. The ordinary folk, not burdened by the pretensions of the better-off, thoroughly enjoyed themselves in an uninhibited manner. Some set up stalls from which they sold gingerbread, coconuts, mangoes, etc; competing loudly and vigorously with each other for customers. The young women openly admired the spirited, youthful, fun-loving midshipmen of Admiral Duckworth's squadron. Ainslie wished with all his heart to join in the fun, but he had to do duty as Miss Baillie's escort.

After the review, a banquet was held in the cool and well-ventilated hall of the Court House, presided over by Custos Stewart. The hall was filled with a large gathering of the landed gentry and the cream of Trelawny and St. James society. The usual speeches and toasts were made, and when it was all over, the guests departed to refresh themselves and prepare for the grand ball.

The saloons and hall of the Court House were brilliantly illuminated for the ball, and when Governor Nugent and his party arrived, the band of the 55th struck up the National Anthem. Dancing began, mostly country dances and highland reels. The enthusiastic crowd danced energetically into the early hours of the morning.

Philip Ainslie took up his job as a bookkeeper on Retirement Estate in St. James. In those days the law required every European male between the ages of sixteen and sixty to join the militia regiment of his parish of residence. Ainslie was enrolled as a private in the Midland Company of the St. James Regiment. One day, while marching with his company to Montego Bay to take part in a parade, he passed many new graves. Buried in them were soldiers of the 55th who had been quartered at the barracks in Montego Bay. In his memoirs, Ainslie wrote that they had soon become sickly, and "many of those stout, healthy men (he) had seen in the fullness of energy on landing at Falmouth" now lay in the graves he had passed, stricken by yellow fever.

Riding on the high road from Retirement Estate to Montego Bay, Ainslie frequently met privates of the 55th, walking from the Montego Bay barracks to Maroon Town. They were orderlies, carrying letters and dispatches. They had to make the journey on foot, to and from Maroon Town, within a certain time, or be punished. "It was sad to see the poor fellows," said Ainslie, "toiling along under the fierce blaze of the tropical sun," wearing the same uniform and equipment they would have worn in England, with the addition of a heavy bag of letters and dispatches. He thought that this "unnecessary hardship" was the cause of much sickness and death among the 55th at Montego Bay; and that it would have been better to let slaves carry the mail.

One day in this period, when a ceremonial salute was being fired at Fort Balcarres, one of the guns exploded, killing two soldiers.

On May 16, 1803, Britain declared war on France, which was then ruled by Napoleon Bonaparte. A French fleet in the

Mediterranean was blockaded by Horatio Nelson, to prevent it from joining a naval concentration in the Atlantic, which would have given Napoleon control of the English Channel.

After being bottled up for two years, the French Mediterranean Fleet escaped, and headed for the West Indies, with Nelson in chase. During this time, shipping around the coast of Jamaica was frequently attacked by French privateers. The north coast was particularly vulnerable. Almost everyday, reports came in of cargo and passenger ships in desperate fights with daring French raiders. Often, ships were captured and re-captured. Sometimes, the privateers landed and plundered houses near the coast.

In July, 1805, *The Royal Gazette* reported that "the south side ports to the leeward of Kingston, from Portland Point to the West end, (were) completely in a state of blockade by the enemy's privateers. Not a single vessel can stir out without the most imminent risk of capture. And not a day passes but these marauders are seen, parading the coast with impunity."

When the French fleet from the Mediterranean arrived in the Caribbean, there was great consternation. It was confidently expected that Jamaica would be invaded. The Governor (General Nugent) held a Council of War in the Kingston Court House, and martial law was proclaimed. Every port in the island was put in the best possible state of defence.

Falmouth was chosen as a site for troop concentration. At 5 o' clock on the morning of April 2, a general muster of the Trelawny Regiment took place at the review ground. At 10 o'clock, three hundred and fifty men of the 55th under the command of Major Chalmers, coming from Maroon Town, entered Falmouth with band playing and colours flying. It was a thrilling sight, but behind the beating drums and the disciplined ranks of redcoats loomed the terrible threat of French invasion.

A few days later, detachments of the 55th from Savanna-la-mar and Lucea arrived in Montego Bay. They were joined by a detachment from the Black Grounds. In company with the detachment stationed at Montego Bay, all marched to Falmouth.

When people saw them marching by, a rumour spread that the French troops had landed to Windward (on the eastern side). Many began packing their valuables and making preparations to send them into the interior of St. James.

With the arrival of the additional detachments from Montego Bay, the entire 55th Regiment, of nearly seven hundred men, was now in Falmouth. The Trelawny Militia, fully armed and ready to fight, was also quartered in the town. There were more than forty ships in the harbour and the captains and crews volunteered their services. The ships were moored in a line across the harbour, forming a battery of between eighty and a hundred guns. Excitement ran high.

In addition to the guns of the ships and the guns of the fort, batteries of heavy artillery were erected in "every eligible situation." Two furnaces for producing red-hot shot were also set up. The use of red-hot shot against wooden ships was a terrible weapon in those days. The rules of war allowed forts to use red hot shot for defence, but denied it to a warship, which was regarded as an aggressor.

Behind this array of armaments, the citizens of Falmouth considered themselves "adequate to resist any attempt of the enemy." Every morning and evening, a general muster of the militia took place on the review ground. Falmouth was bursting at the seams with armed men.

Late on Thursday night, April 11, an alarm was given when a gun was fired from a cruiser out at sea. The drums beat to arms and "the whole of the regulars and the militia were immediately under arms." Falmouth citizens waited tensely. The troops remained under arms until daylight, and hardly anyone in the town slept that night. Fortunately, it turned out to be a false alarm.

Late in April, the entire colony was relieved when a British naval squadron arrived in Port Royal with a reinforcement of troops. It was now felt that martial law was no longer necessary, and it was discontinued, after having been in force for nineteen days. Shortly after, news came that the French fleet had attacked and ravaged Dominica, but had been forced to withdraw before an advancing British naval squadron. The period of extreme tension and excitement in Falmouth was over. On the morning of April 23, one company of the 55$^{th}$ embarked for Montego Bay, and two companies for Lucea and Savanna-la-Mar. At four in the afternoon, another company marched out of town for the Black Grounds, and five other companies under Major Chalmers, marched for Maroon Town, led by the band of music.

All was not yet over. Martial Law was again proclaimed in May, when it was reported that seventeen French ships were at Martinique. Fortunately, Horatio Nelson with ten ships-of-the-line and three frigates, arrived and chased them away. However, the coasts of Jamaica and the Windward Passage continued to be harassed by privateers, but with Nelson pursuing the French fleet, it was felt that invasion was no longer probable.

There were now almost five thousand regular troops in Jamaica including five hundred and fifty men of the 2$^{nd}$ West India Regiment. In addition, the island's militia numbered nearly ten thousand foot and one thousand horse.

On May 23, 1805, the transport, Suffolk, arrived in Montego Bay from Port Royal and Port Antonio with recruits for the 55$^{th}$, but the Regiment was approaching the close of its assignment in the west. By July and the early days of August, the men were pulling out of the Black Grounds, Maroon Town, Falmouth, Montego Bay, Lucea and Savanna-la-Mar, and headed for Spanish Town. They were replaced by the 60$^{th}$ Regiment.

After serving in the Leeward posts for a little over three years, the 55$^{th}$, like other regiments before and after them, left tangible reminders of their stay. Many of the men left sweethearts and children behind when they marched away. In fact, in Maroon Town there was a distinct change in the complexion of the inhabitants over the years, as a result of the presence of the British troops up to the 1850s.

Apart from the 83$^{rd}$, 55$^{th}$, and 60$^{th}$, other British regiments were stationed in Falmouth while it was a "Garrison" town. Among them were the 20$^{th}$ Light Dragoons, and the 53$^{rd}$,

37th, 82nd, 68th, 92nd, 33rd, 77th, and 8th regiments. In 1867, the Third West India Regiment was also in town.

Several of the military men married local women. For instance:- Michael White Lee, Captain 55th, married Judith Barrett of St. James, widow, on March 12, 1803.

John Warren, Captain, 92nd Regiment, married Elizabeth Scarlett Innes, spinster, on December 18, 1822.

John Longden, Major 33rd Regiment, married Susan Campbell of Trelawny, spinster, on November 30, 1825. It also appears that the "colour line" in matters of rank and marriage, was sometimes broken or relaxed. For instance:- Richard Parkinson, Corporal, 83rd Regiment, married Anne Page "a person of colour," in 1797.

John Chryster, a 35 year-old Lieutenant, 53rd Regiment, who died and was buried on February 8, 1820, was a "Free Quadroon."

Bathest, a black man, Drummer 92nd Regiment, was married to Mary, a white woman. Their daughter, Elizabeth, and son C.M Bathest, were baptized on March 10, 1822, and September 5, 1823.

In May 1808, a little over three years after the time of "The French Scare," a dreadful fire broke out in Falmouth, which nearly destroyed the town. More than fifty houses were burnt. The most valuable of these buildings stood on Market Street, and were stored with recently imported goods. They were entirely consumed by the fire, except for the walls.

The warship H.M.S. Favourite, commanded by Captain Clement, was in port. Clement and his officers and men, together with the captains and crews of several merchant vessels in the harbour, fought the fire with every resource at their disposal, and probably saved the town. The people of Falmouth expressed their deep gratitude to the officers and sailors for their "indefatigable exertions" in fighting the fire. Fortunately, no lives were lost.

# THE TRELAWNY MILITIA

The Trelawny Militia Regiment was said to have been more highly honoured by the respective Governors of Jamaica and their ladies, than any other on the island. In the early 1800s, it was made up of ten battalion companies and an artillery company.

In November 1821, the regiment (commanded by Colonel Miller) and the Squadron of Horse (under Captain Earnshaw) were inspected by Major-General Fairclough at the muster ground just outside of Falmouth. According to a report in the Supplement to the Royal Gazette of December 1-8, 1821:

> *The movements of the infantry, and firings by volleys and companies were executed with that steadiness and correctness for which the Regiment has been long eminent, and which, we think, can only be surpassed by regular troops.*
>
> *The very handsome terms in which the General expressed to Colonel Miller his most unqualified approbation at the high state of discipline and performances of this fine corps, fully justify the foregoing remark, and demonstrate that the Trelawny Regiment maintains the character it has successively and deservedly possessed – of being the best Militia Regiment in the island.*
>
> *The excellent state of the arms and accoutrements, as well as the uniform, clean, appearance of the men, did not escape the General's observation.*
>
> *The charges and evolution of the squadron (of Horse) merited the eulogium likewise bestowed upon it by the Inspector General. Both troops were, with but two or three exceptions, remarkably well mounted.*

> *In the evening, the General and his suite, with many civil and military guests, honoured the Officers of the Regiment and troops with their company at the Court House for dinner, where wines in great variety, and of the choicest quality, were introduced.*
>
> *Loyal and patriotic toasts were "drank" to the King, the Royal Family, the Duke of York and the Army, the Duke of Clarence and the Navy, the Lieutenant Governor, the absent Governor, the island of Jamaica, the Commander in Chief and the Forces in the island, etc.*

The Regimental Band played appropriate tunes after each toast, "and the company retired at about 2 o'clock in the morning, highly gratified with the entertainment, if we may judge from the hilarity and good humour that pervaded the whole."

A few years later, Colonel Miller received his commission of Major General, at the head of the regiment, from the hands of Sir John Keane, the then Governor.

Colonel William Cadien (who commanded the regiment during the Sam Sharpe Rebellion of 1831) was presented with a set of colours by the Countess of Mulgrave for the use of the regiment. The Earl of Mulgrave, during his time as Governor, repeatedly reviewed the regiment "and mixed in social intercourse with the respectable inhabitants of the parish, which he visited frequently."

It was reported, however, that Governor Sir Lionel Smith, while reviewing the regiment, saw a militiaman with a very large paunch. To the surprise of everyone, Sir Lionel asked the portly fellow how he managed to carry around such a big bag of tripe.

On Saturday, May 5, 1852, the Trelawny Leeward Troop of the Western Division of Horse disgraced itself. Fifty-seven years earlier, in 1795, the troop had been part of the contingent which had ridden behind Colonel Sandford into the "Valley of Death" (between the Old and New Maroon Towns), where they had been ambushed by the Trelawny Maroons and suffered numerous casualties. Now in 1852, some two or three generations later, when the Troop was ordered by its captain to muster on May 1, the order was ignored. Captain Isaacs and the trumpeter were the only ones who turned up on the field.

The angry captain planned to issue warrants against the absentees for not appearing armed and accoutred according to law; but apparently never did so.

Times had changed. The Maroons were now peaceful, and slavery had been abolished. The need for the troop to keep in tip-top shape, and, indeed, the main reason for the existence of the Jamaica Militia, of which they were a part, had largely disappeared. The Militia was replaced not long after by volunteer groups in most parishes. Trelawny, Kingston, and Spanish Town were regarded as having the best volunteer contingents.

The Trelawny Volunteer Corps, under Captain Frederick Lindo, mustered in full force for a rifle-shooting contest on Thursday, February 4, 1864, at the Parade Ground, before a large gathering of people. The first prize was an "excellent revolver" donated by William Sewell, for the best shot at 150, 200, 250, and 300 yards; five shots each. It was won by Duncan Pasmore. The second prize, a handsome candelabra subscribed by the Volunteers themselves, was won by Jacob Reuben. The contest began at midday and ended at 6pm. At one point, a concert of 'popular airs' was given by the volunteer band under the leadership of Simon Perez. An observer noticed, with great pleasure, "the improvement that had been made by each member of the band".

On Friday, October 7, 1864 the Volunteers celebrated their second anniversary at the Court House. Their commander was still Captain Frederick Lindo. Nearly two years later, on August 21, 1866, they took on the 2nd West India Regiment in a rifle shooting contest and were beaten. The Voluntcers struggled on for a few more years, but began to disintegrate when Frederick Lindo left the parish.

## **WILLIAM KNIBB & THE BAPTIST WAR**

Religion came officially to Trelawny when the Parish church was opened in 1796. It was, of course, an Anglican church, an arm of the established religion. Accordingly, it was conservative and supportive of the Planters and the status quo. Up to 1836 (as in England), people could only be legally married by an Anglican clergyman.

The Baptist faith was brought to Jamaica in about 1783 by George Leile, a freed American slave. Leile's people were called "Native Baptists". Except for these "Native Baptists", the churches were very careful not to annoy slave owners. If they interfered with slavery, the Planters would prevent them from preaching to their slaves, and might even drive them out of the country since they controlled the Government.

Specific instructions were given to missionaries and teachers who were being sent to Jamaica. They must have nothing to do with civil or political matters. Not a word must be said by them in public or private, which might make the slaves displeased with their masters or dissatisfied with their condition. They were not being sent to relieve the slaves from their condition, but to give them the consolation of religion, and enforce on them the necessity of being subject. Their solemn duty was to teach the slave obedience to his master and his God. They must not incur the displeasure of the slave owners. On the contrary, they must placate them and not endanger the public peace and safety. What is preached must make the slaves more diligent, faithful, patient and useful, whether their masters were gentle, or whether they were harsh. In that way, they would please even those who were against the teaching of religion to the slaves.

These "Instructions" placed a great burden on missionaries and teachers who were horrified by slavery. They were forced to be silent and to steel their hearts, even in the face of what was cruel and revolting. The "Native Baptists" however, were not burdened by this painful hypocrisy. They went steadily about their work, and, as a result, soon ran into all kinds of trouble. Eventually, laws were passed which prevented them from openly preaching to slaves.

They appealed to the Baptists in Britain for help, and English missionaries and teachers were sent out to assist them; bound by instructions to extremely limited activities. The first English Baptist missionary to come to Jamaica was John Rowe, who brought the Baptist church to Falmouth in 1814.

Rowe died of yellow fever in 1816, and the Falmouth Baptists had no minister until 1827, when Thomas Burchell arrived. Burchell firmly established the church, and when he left, James Mann took over; but Mann died in 1830, and the Falmouth Baptists had to look around again for a new minister.

William Knibb had meanwhile come to Jamaica to take the place of his brother Thomas, who had died while teaching at a Baptist school in Kingston. Knibb and his wife, Mary, arrived at the Baptist Mission House on East Queen Street in Kingston on February 12, 1825. Knibb was the fifth of eight children (born with his twin sister Ann) and his father was a tradesman.

In spite of the "Instructions" not to get involved with things in Jamaica, Knibb wrote his mother after a few weeks to say that "the cursed blast of slavery" was like a pestilence which withered every moral bloom… "I know not how any person can find a union with such a demon, such a child of hell… for myself, I feel a burning hatred against it."

To his brother Edward, he wrote: "the more I see of slavery, the more I hate and abhor it. [You must never] argue in support of such a system so repugnant to every feeling of Right and Justice."

It soon became obvious that Knibb had a gift for preaching. Rev. James Coultart, the missionary in charge of the East Queen Street Baptist Church, asked him to preach. When Knibb visited the western end of the island, Rev. Thomas Burchell also asked him to preach, but in preaching, Knibb was breaking the law. Non-conformists, such as Baptists, Methodists, Moravians and Presbyterians, were not allowed to preach without a licence. Knibb had no licence.

Before he could apply for a licence, he had to get the approval of the Baptist Missionary Society in England. They didn't think he had the necessary academic training; but when the missionaries in Jamaica wrote supporting his application, they gave permission.

In 1829, Knibb resigned his teaching job when he was invited to Ridgeland, near Savanna-la-Mar in Westmoreland, to do missionary work. One of his deacons in the Ridgeland church was a slave named Sam Swiney, who was asked to gather people in the mission house one day, for a prayer meeting. In the midst of prayers, an officer of the law walked in and arrested Swiney for preaching. A law said that slaves who preached or taught without the permission of their owners would be whipped or imprisoned in the work house at hard labour. Witnesses testified that Swiney was praying and not preaching, but the magistrates sentenced him to both whipping and the treadmill.

It was Knibb's first real test. Should he look the other way and avoid angering the authorities? He reported the matter to the Baptist Missionary Society in England and sent an appeal to the Secretary of State for the Colonies. It took two years before a decision was received. The action of the magistrates in sentencing Swiney to both whipping and the treadmill was found to be illegal. The magistrates were dismissed and told to return to England.

Knibb had begun to build a reputation for himself as a man of courage, who was committed to justice. When James Mann, Minister of the Falmouth Baptist Church died in 1830, a church meeting was called to decide on a replacement. Thomas Burchell nominated William Knibb for the post and asked for a show of hands. The entire gathering rose to their feet, lifted their hands, and gave spontaneous and joyful approval. All wept openly.

Knibb arrived in Falmouth with his wife and two children in June, 1830. He threw himself into the work at once. His mission stations were numerous and far apart, and he was still serving churches in Westmoreland which were eighty-six miles away by horseback.

On Sundays, he held three services in Falmouth. On Tuesdays, he rode to Oxford and Cambridge estates, where the proprietor allowed him to teach the slaves. On Wednesdays, he went to Rio Bueno, and on Saturdays to Stewart Town, where he corrected "faults", held baptisms, etc. Sometimes he was completely exhausted. All the while, he kept fairly rigidly to the missionary "Instructions" not to get involved in secular matters, and he dutifully demanded that the members of his church be obedient to their masters.

About a year and six months after his arrival in Falmouth, a massive slave uprising took place on December 27, 1831, in neighbouring St. James. It was called "the Baptist War" since the vast majority of the slaves involved appeared to be Baptists. It turned out to be the last slave rebellion in Jamaica, and it was led by a house slave from Montego Bay named Samuel Sharpe, who was a Baptist deacon.

The insurrection spread rapidly in western parishes, including Trelawny. Its message was loud, clear and revolutionary. No more work without pay. If the rebels won their demand it would put an end to slavery in Jamaica. The uprising started as a peaceful movement, but militants took over and about one hundred and seventy properties were set on fire. The frightened Planters believed that Non-conformist missionaries, especially Baptists, had incited the slaves to rebel. They began to persecute missionaries even as the country threw all its armed might against the rebels.

Knibb and other missionaries were in Falmouth when martial law was proclaimed on Saturday, December 31, 1831. They feared that military rule would lay them wide open to attack. A soldier entered Knibb's yard and seized a saddle for "the service of the King" and the anxiety of the missionaries grew when they saw captured slaves being led past their houses to the jail. On the morning of Sunday, January 1, 1832, Knibb held two public prayer meetings at his chapel. After the second meeting, a non-commissioned officer named Denoon, accompanied by four soldiers armed with guns and fixed bayonets, rounded up Knibb and his fellow missionaries: Whitehorn, Nichols and Abbott. Whitehorn and Nichols were escorted to the Guard House and Knibb and Abbott were ordered to present themselves there.

At the Guard House, the four missionaries waited in the officers' apartment for over an hour to see Lieutenant-Colonel Cadien. At the end of that time, Major Robert Neilson entered and thanked them for attending so promptly. He asked them to report back every morning at eleven so as to set a good example to others, and until orders were received from the Commander-in-Chief, Major General, Sir Willoughby Cotton, indicating how they should be treated. Both Denoon and Neilson had been quite polite, and the missionaries returned to their families rejoicing that nothing terrible had happened.

The next day, they waited for an hour at the Guard Room, then Cadien himself appeared and told them quite bluntly that: "They had better join themselves to some company." The missionaries were astonished that they were being literally ordered to join the Militia. They said they had been under the impression that all Ministers of the Gospel were exempt from military service; but Cadien made it plain that he meant what he said.

Abbott joined the Artillery Company. Knibb joined the Fourth Company under Captain Chrystie. Whitehorn asked that his former rank of Captain be restored and was instructed to send for his commission. Nichols fell ill and was given a passport to return to St. Ann's Bay.

Knibb and Abbott went on guard duty at 5pm that day. Knibb soon felt sick and was allowed to go home; but poor Abbott spent from 10pm to 1am pacing about as a sentry. For the remainder of the night, he tried to rest on a table in the Guard Room, but was kept awake by the "filthy" conversation of the Militiamen. On Tuesday, January 3, Knibb and Abbott wrote a letter to the Governor asking for exemption from military service. They gave it to Cadien for inspection before sending it off to Spanish Town which was then the capital of Jamaica. Cadien promised to give them his opinion before noon. They waited anxiously.

Suddenly, Captain Paul Doig of the Sixth Battalion Company burst in with drawn sword, accompanied by two armed soldiers. Pointing his sword at Knibb he said in a harsh voice: "Take this man into custody. This is all he has got by preaching." Knibb was shocked. Years later he wrote:

> *I was arrested in the most brutal manner by a man named Paul Doig... He paraded before me in all the pomp of petty power, with a drawn sword.*

Knibb was taken to the ballroom upstairs the Court House, which was being used as a barrack. He was left there guarded by a sentry. Captain Chrystie went to Abbott and quite politely asked him to deliver up his sword, as the Colonel had ordered his arrest. Abbott was taken to the ballroom. Whitchorn, hearing that his colleagues had been arrested, went to them and was detained by the sentry.

An hour or two later, Captain Chrystie informed them that Cadien had received word from Montego Bay and was sending them to the headquarters there in half an hour's time. They were not allowed to see their wives or write letters, but were permitted to make a list of things they would require in the canoe which would take them to Montego Bay. They sent a message to their wives to meet them there. At 11:30 am, accompanied by a large crowd of friends and foes, they were marched through the streets under a military guard, to a wharf some distance from the Court House.

The canoe put to sea at about twenty minutes to twelve under a boiling sun. After seven hours, they reached Montego Bay, which was in turmoil. Two warships were lying near the town, guard boats were going back and forth, houses were burning on neighbouring hills and musket fire was heard from further inland. Knibb and his colleagues were marched to the Court House, then to General Cotton's lodgings, then back to the Court House, then to Custos Barrett's house (half a mile away), and back to the Court House again, carrying their luggage all the way, and taunted by passersby.

At the Court House, they were surrounded by officers and men using threatening language. After being exposed in a witness box for some time, they were taken to the Customs House. The next morning, they were released by Custos Barrett on a fifty-pound bail, with the understanding that they would not leave Montego Bay and would appear when called.

It had been a terrifying and most humiliating experience, but that was the mood of the country, as it was represented by the Planters and their supporters. In the process, William Knibb had learned a hard lesson: that it was not possible for people who believed in freedom and human dignity to make accommodation with the existing system of slavery. This was something that Sam Sharpe and his followers had realized some time before, which had led them to put their lives at risk in the cause of liberty. At least five hundred of them were to pay with their lives, but their bold action did more than any single thing to speed-up the coming of freedom.

# THE END OF SLAVERY

Trouble broke out in Trelawny among the slaves on Pantrepant, Golden Grove, Carrickfoyle and other estates. Two divisions of the Trelawny Regiment, with a few regular soldiers, took up positions at Bounty Hall and Good Hope estates, and in a few days sent in two hundred prisoners. The Clarendon militia was ordered into the parish to assist the Trelawny Regiment, and a detachment of the Kingston Regiment was alerted to proceed there. Charles Town and Moore Town Maroons volunteered to serve in Trelawny, and a ship from Port Antonio took fifty from each town to Falmouth.

Cadien, now made a full Colonel, was ordered to move from Falmouth to Spring Vale in St. James. A few days later, the entire strength of the Trelawny Regiment was on duty in that parish. Towards the end of January 1832, it became obvious that the back of the rebellion was broken. It was also time to begin reaping the sugar crop. Cadien was asked to send the overseers and bookkeepers in his regiment back to the estates in Trelawny where they were employed, so they could commence the crop.

The Trelawny Regiment and the St. Ann Western Regiment were ordered to march to Montego Bay. The day before the Trelawny militiamen had marched about fifty miles through the woods "and every inch of it on foot". Cadien had six hundred and eight men, including 52 mounted troopers and 40 Regulars. When they arrived in Montego Bay with the St. Ann Western Regiment, they were formed up in divisions in front of the court house. After giving three hearty cheers, they were dismissed, and "all appeared in excellent health".

Less than two weeks earlier, on January 26, some Planters and their supporters formed an organization in St. Ann's Bay called the Colonial Church Union. The founder was an Anglican clergyman: Rev. George Wilson Bridges, Rector of St. Ann. The Union's main purpose was to maintain the institution of slavery, and, in so doing, to harass and terrorize the non-conformist faiths, especially the Baptists and Methodists, who were seen as enemies of slavery.

The Colonial Church Union recruited most of its members from the ranks of the Militia, and it had branches all over the island. It didn't take hold in Kingston, however, because of the militant mood of the large, well-organized Non-conformist population there.

On their way home from Montego Bay, elements of the St. Ann Regiment stopped in Falmouth to wreck Non-conformist chapels, which they regarded as the dens of the enemy. Knibb's church was demolished, and on the night of February 7, St. Ann Militiamen began tearing down the Methodist chapel which had just been repaired. They didn't complete the job but took away much of the material they had torn down.

A few nights later, a mob of troopers from the Trelawny Regiment, assisted by sailors from ships in the habour under their captains, and by some of the inhabitants of the town, began to complete the work of destroying the Methodist chapel. They used axes and ropes, and blocks supplied from the ships. Some Militia officers stationed in Falmouth tried to intervene, but the magistrates refused to assert their authority. Instead, they sanctioned the activities of the wreckers and encouraged them.

The wrecking operations were brought to a fitting close when a vandal went late at night to steal loose pieces of timber from the ruins. A large portion of the upper floor had escaped demolition, and while removing boards from this section, the vandal pulled down the whole thing on himself. The next morning, he was discovered with his neck broken by the end of a large beam, which had fallen on him and pinned him to the earth.

In addition to the Baptist and Methodist chapels in Falmouth, the Stewart Town Chapel was destroyed by fire. The Grenadier Company of the Trelawny Regiment, dressed in their uniforms, attacked the chapel at Rio Bueno which was strongly built of stone. After two attempts, they succeeded in demolishing it.

William Knibb went to England to report what had taken place to the Baptist Missionary Society and to press for the abolition of slavery. He openly declared that he would not rest, day or night, until he saw slavery destroyed "root and branch".

Knibb spoke at a large public meeting and was sent on a lecture tour throughout Britain. He was called to appear in the House of Commons and attended for three days. Afterwards, he appeared in the House of Lords. His evidence was considered to be complete and unassailable and it helped to convince the English public that slavery must be abolished.

Burchell joined Knibb in England. While both were still there, a bill to abolish slavery was introduced into the British Parliament in July 1833, and was passed in August.

The bill declared that slavery was to cease on August 1, 1834. So it was that Trelawny and Falmouth, through the Baptist giant, William Knibb, became associated with events that led to the abolition of slavery, not only in Jamaica, but throughout the British Empire.

# THE BLACK BLOOD OF BLEBY

Among the people who were fascinated by Samuel Sharpe, the paramount leader of the Baptist slave uprising of 1831 was Rev. Henry Bleby, a Methodist minister.

Bleby witnessed Sharpe's execution in the Montego Bay market square. He was awed by Sharpe's tremendous dignity and strength, and was almost anxious to see how he would face death.

When the execution was over, Bleby turned away and wiped tears from his eyes. He was overcome with deep sorrow and indignation "that such a man as Samuel Sharpe should be thus immolated at the polluted shrine of slavery".

Shortly after martial law came to an end, the pro-slavery Colonial Church Union began to attack missionaries and their congregations, and to wreck and burn Baptist and Methodist chapels.

Bleby was having tea in his house in Falmouth when a mob broke through his gate, smashed the windows of the house and burst open the front door. Some of them ran upstairs and grabbed Bleby. A man named Dobson hit him on the head with a stick, and he was held by the arms and collar and pinioned against a window frame.

Somebody brought in a keg of tar and several of Bleby's assailants dipped their hands in it and smeared tar over his head, face and upper body. Some of it was rubbed into his eyes and soon tar was running down his trousers to the floor. Dobson took a lighted candle to set fire to him but

Mrs. Bleby, who was an extraordinary woman, kicked the candle from his hand as he bent down to apply the flame to Bleby's trouser leg. Mrs. Bleby was pulled away, thrown upon the floor and trampled.

There was another candle burning in the room. Dobson got it and was about to apply the flame to Bleby's neck cloth when Mrs. Bleby scrambled up from the floor and knocked it away. The candle went out and the room was in darkness except for the moonlight. Mrs. Bleby was dragged off again and pushed into a closet just outside the sitting room door.

Just then, the Bleby's five-month old son, who had been sleeping on the couch throughout all the turmoil, awoke and began to cry. The leader of the mob ordered the child to be thrown out of the window. Mrs. Bleby, breaking out somehow, dashed into the room, grabbed the child and ran with it through the back door.

Meanwhile, the news had spread that the Bleby's house was under attack, and a group of black and brown men came into the yard. They armed themselves with clubs from a bundle of fire wood, and fell upon the Union ruffians who were in the lower part of the house. Those upstairs heard the commotion and fled. Bleby, covered with tar, started to go downstairs and came face to face with Dobson. Dobson swung at him with a stick and Bleby ran back upstairs. He had a pistol up there but couldn't bring himself to use it. Apparently, no one followed him upstairs, so after awhile, he went down cautiously into the yard.

Union bullies were still in the yard and some of them rushed him. The men who had come to his rescue pushed him into their midst and met the charge of the Union men "hand to hand". The Union attackers were driven back and Bleby was helped to escape over a fence. Shortly after, he found his courageous wife with the baby in her arms, near the ruins of the Falmouth chapel.

The drops of tar, which had dripped from Bleby during the attempt to lynch him, dried on the floor of the house. Many scrubbings failed to remove them.

More than sixty years later, when the Chief Clerk of the Trelawny Parochial Board (William Fitz-Ritson) was living in the house with his family, the black drops were still on the floor. The children were told the story about the attack by the Union men in 1832; but somebody got the facts a little wrong. The children got the impression that Bleby had been severely wounded, or killed; and that the black drops on the floor had been made by his dripping blood. It certainly was more "fun" to think of the black drops in that way.

## THE MAVERICK OF THE HOUSE OF REID

*(According to the dictionary a Maverick is someone who exhibits great independence in thought and action. Independent in behavior or thought)*

In a private cemetery on the grounds of Good Hope Estate is the tomb of a man named Thomas Reid.

Thomas Reid was the grandson of William Reid, a member of the Assembly, who was given a patent of land by Queen Anne of England in 1709. The Land lay in the Queen of Spain's Valley in today's parish of Trelawny. It developed into Long Pond Sugar Estate.

William Reid and his family were driven from the Queen of Spain's Valley by Cudjoe's Maroons in 1735. They took refuge in neighbouring St. Ann. Along with other settlers, they fought hard against the Maroons. At the end of the war the assembly voted a sum of money to one of William's sons (known in family lore as Ranger John), for his extraordinary services and his sufferings.

The British establishment was twice forced to come to terms with spirited elements in the African population of Jamaica (first the Spanish African Juan de Bolas in 1663, and then Cudjoe in 1739). In a similar way some families like the Reids, developed a kinship with people who worked in bondage on their plantations.

William Reid died in 1741. In his will he freed his "wench", Kate, and all her mulatto children and also a mulatto girl child belonging to Maria (Kate may have been the Indian Catherine mentioned in an earlier Reid document. Maria could have been Hispanic).

Among the freed children of "colour" living on William Reid's estates, was a girl named Catherine who was about

3 years old when he died. Her father was one of William's sons, known in the family as Junior William (he was also a member of the assembly). Catherine was strongly attached to her Reid heritage, and refused to be defined by anything else.

When Junior William died in 1763, he left two properties: Friendship and Studley Park, to his three surviving sons (George, Thomas & John-not to be confused with Ranger). Thomas was 11 when Junior William died. The name Studley Park was changed to Bunkers Hill in 1777, about 2 years after the battle of Bunkers Hill, which was one of the earlier battles in the American war of Independence. This gave the impression that either one of the Reids or a friend of the family, took part in the battle of Bunkers Hill.

Thomas and his brother John inherited Bunkers Hill, but apparently Thomas was not a good manager and after a while, he was forced to turn over his half of Bunkers Hill to his brothers. Thomas had married one of the daughters of the well known Haughton-James family. She died childless at about the time when he was losing Bunkers Hill.

Thomas' brothers, George and John, went to live in England as absentee landlords, one in St. Pancras, and the other at St. Giles-in-the-field, in the county of Middlesex. They entered into the world so brilliantly described by Jane Austen in such novels as Pride and Prejudice. George's son married the fourth daughter of Sir Charles Oakley (Baronet) and thus entered the fringes of the British aristocracy.

Thomas after a brief stay in England, returned to Jamaica and moved to St Ann, where his grandfather had taken refuge from the Maroons in 1735. He may have made the move because of the slave rebellion which broke out in Trelawny in 1797.

Thomas set up house with a lady of colour. She bore him a daughter in 1805 who was named Mary and a son in 1811 christened John.

People of colour, the off-spring of British fathers and women of African or Indian decent, were often greatly loved by their fathers, who sometimes left them significant sums of money and much land. Many were sent to England or Europe to be educated. Some never returned as they were better treated abroad. They were becoming so wealthy that conservative elements among the ruling class passed laws to limit what they could inherit.

Respectable members of the ruling class were not expected to openly associate with their children of colour, or even ride in a carriage with them. Thomas Reid defied such social practices and openly embraced his two children of colour (Mary and John) as his personal family.

Thomas was a proud stubborn man, very much aware of his Reid heritage in Jamaica going back to the old Port Royal days before the earthquake, when his great grandfather had been a member of the assembly and for a brief while, a member of the Governor's Council. He was also Advocate General in the Court of Admiralty at Port Royal and an acquaintance of the great buccaneer Henry Morgan.

Thomas often signed his name with the one word REID, as if he represented in himself all that the name stood for. The remote roots of the Reids lay in Colliston, in Angus, on the east coast of Scotland.

Thomas was 53 when his daughter Mary was born. He and his half-sister Catherine, child of his father (Junior William) were very good friends, and they had a lot in common. Both were able to carve out a rugged freedom for themselves in the society.

Catherine became the housekeeper (which usually meant unofficial wife) of a well-to-do man of colour named Neil. When Catherine was about 43 or 44 she gave birth to a son for Neil, who was sent as a boy to England to be educated.

Neil bought a 50 acre property called Epsom Pen. When he died he left Epsom to Catherine for her lifetime. When she died the property was to go to her son, and, if he died before Catherine, Epsom was to go to the survivors of Neil's other children by other women. At the age of 61, Catherine got married to a man named Wyatt and went to England to organize, with the help of her half-brothers, a marriage settlement to ensure that nobody, including her husband could get their hands on her property. Unfortunately for Catherine her son died shortly after he returned to Jamaica, so the property would have to go on her death to the survivors of Neil's other children.

Catherine's husband Mr. Wyatt also died and was buried at Epsom. With his death she drew closer and closer to her niece and nephew, Mary and John, the children of her half brother Thomas. She invited John to be the overseer at Epsom, and asked Mary to come and live with her.

While at Epsom, Mary met Paul Doig who lived at Hammersmith on the border of Epsom. He was born in Scotland at Murdiston Farm, near Thorn Hill in South Perthshire. As Captain in the Trelawny Militia, Doig arrested William Knibb during the Sam Sharpe rebellion 1831-32. He and Mary became romantically involved, so they put together an establishment and started having children. Doig became restless because his future seemed uncertain; so he went to Scotland and then accompanied members of his family who were migrating to Canada. There he ran into long cold winters and deep snows and after a while, his thoughts began turning to Jamaica and to Mary.

In 1834 just before she died, Catherine, ignoring the terms of Neil's will, left Epsom for Mary and John. In the meantime, hearing of Catherine's death, the heirs of Neil demanded that Epsom be turned over to them. When nothing much appeared to be happening, they placed the matter into the hands of William Miller, an influential Magistrate who lived near Epsom.

Miller went to Epsom and threatened to sue John for rent owing to his clients from the time of Catherine's death. Miller installed his own overseer at Epsom and John left.

At first, Miller allowed the Reid's livestock, furniture and apprentices to remain at Epsom. When it became apparent that Mary was making no effort to remove her family's belongings, or the workers for whom the Reids were responsible, Miller decided to take action. On Tuesday, February 24th, 1837, he entered Epsom with a gang of workers who went into the house and started to throw out the Reid's possessions. In the midst of the turmoil Mary arrived.

"Remove your belongings from this property," Miller told her.

"I have no place to take them", she said.

"I don't care." replied Miller, People who have no place, ought to have nothing."

Mary moved out all her furniture except the things in her father's room. She sent a message at once to her father Thomas, asking for help. She also sent a message to William Tharpe, one of Catherine's executors, asking him to intervene.

Thomas didn't hesitate. At the age of about 86, he left his home in St. Ann on February 27th, 1837, in his carriage (it was described as a gig) with two of his servants, John Campbell and Dennis Reid, and headed for Epsom.

He arrived at Epsom Pen on Sunday, February 29th. The roads being what they were in those days, it had taken him all that time to get to Epsom. The gate into Epsom was locked. Miller's overseer was away at the time, and had left the gate key with a female apprentice, instructing her to not to give the key to anyone, and not to open the gate.

The old patriarch was in his carriage outside the gate; How could she keep him locked out? Intimidated, she handed over the key.

Thomas was driven up to the house. He was in the act of climbing up the steps, when he was told that his daughter was at Hammersmith. On his way out of Epsom, Thomas threw away the gate key. Nobody was going to lock him out again. Mary was at Hammersmith, three-quarters of a mile away. She told him what happened. He asked her to send some dinner for him at Epsom, bought a new lock and key for the Epsom gate and drove back up the hill. When he went through the gate he put on the new lock.

Thomas sat down in the house and had the dinner which Mary had sent.

He had scarcely finished eating before he heard a terrible knocking at the gate. A gang of men was at the gate headed by Miller's overseer. Thomas went into the yard.

They demanded the key. Thomas refused. They broke the lock and rushed in.

At this point a message arrived from William Tharpe who advised Thomas to remain where he was until morning, when he would come over to see him in possession. When the gang heard this they quieted down.

Thomas went back to the house, which was full of people. Exhausted, he went to his room and threw himself on his bed in his clothes.

Mary arrived shortly after. On her way into the yard she noticed that her father's gig had been taken out into the road. When one of the servants tried to bring it back he was prevented.

A message was sent to William Miller to let him know what was happening.

Miller arrived around 10 pm. He was accompanied by a friend named Frederick Coore.

"Who is here?" asked Miller. Someone told him Mr. Reid from St. Ann was inside.

Thomas heard heavy footsteps, which advanced into his room.

He said:-

"Who is that?" Miller and Coore entered the room.

"My name is William Miller and this is Mr. Coore," said Miller.

"What do you want?" Thomas enquired.

" I've come to turn you out. I wonder how such an old man as you can be so impudent as to give me so much trouble."

Thomas said " I will meet you in the morning at Falmouth, and we will settle the business there."

"No I have come to turn you out," Miller insisted. " you shall not remain another minute."

"I will not go out. Sooner than I go I will have a musket ball through my breast. You will have to take me out dead."

"I won't kill you." Miller said, "but I'll put you out easy enough."

By now Mary was in the room. Miller grabbed Thomas and gave him a "confounded shake" and started dragging him off the bed. But it wasn't as easy as Miller thought it would be. Turning to Coore he said;

" Mr. Coore, I wish you would assist me in taking out this old gentleman."

Coore laid hold of Thomas on one side. They didn't lift him off the ground, but they "armed" him out of the house and carried him out faster than he could walk. Mary began to cry. Miller turned to her and said

"My good woman, you shall quit Hammersmith tomorrow, or your things shall be sold for house rent."

Miller and Coore dragged Thomas about three hundred yards down the avenue, leading from Epsom House to the Kings Road; down Green Park Way. They lugged him out very roughly, and his coat and shirt were torn in the process. Dennis Reid, Thomas' servant, followed close behind them with a light. Mary remained behind to take care of a few things. She sent for her father's horses from the pasture, as Miller had threatened to send them to the pound. Then she hurried down the road, a little distance behind.

When they reached an old cotton tree Miller became exhausted. He said to Coore:

"Let the old rascal go and find an asylum where he can."

They let Thomas go, and Coore began to feel ashamed about the whole thing.

"I will lend you my pony." Coore said to Thomas. " he's a quiet beast and will take you to Hammersmith."

But Thomas refused the offer. So they went off and left him by the old cotton tree. Dennis his servant helped him to walk the rest of the way to Hammersmith. "He couldn't have made it by himself," Dennis said later, "as he was quite lame and the night was very dark."

Mary, in great distress, returned to Epsom behind Miller and Coore, to finish putting together the things which belonged to her father and herself. She had no doubt now that Miller would destroy her belongings if she didn't get them out of the place. Miller ordered Mary's cattle to be turned out on the King's Road. " I'll give you grass for them until you can sell them," he told her.

Mary said that when Coore reached Epsom and saw Thomas Reid's carriage in the road, he said:

" Had I seen it before we might have had the horses put to it for the old man."

But Miller said:

"Let him find his way in the best manner he can. He has plenty of servants."

That Sunday night of Feb. 29, 1837 was a very low point in Mary's life, as she made her way to Hammersmith in the darkness. Miller's mission on behalf of Neil's heirs appeared to have succeeded, but old Thomas Reid had no thought of giving up. He took the matter to court. Miller also brought an action against him for trespass.

"The case was tried on Tuesday July 4th, and Wednesday July 5th, in the first instance. The presiding judges were the Chief Justice, Sir Joshua Rowe, and Alexander Grant. The case was the King vs. William Miller a gentleman well-known in this parish (Trelawny) and Mr. Frederick Coore, for an aggravated assault upon the person of Mr. Thomas Reid, a man eighty-six years old."

The court felt bound to express their regret that persons in Mr. Miller's and Mr. Coore's station of life should have been guilty of turning a man of the plaintiff's age out of his house at that hour of night. The court felt however, that Miller would not have taken the steps he did, had he not acted under legal advice.

A writer of an editorial in the Falmouth post asked; "What are the facts? A magistrate of the parish of Trelawny, a guardian of the laws enacted for the protection of His Majesty's subjects attended by a host of miscreants in his employ, entered the dwelling of an aged gentleman at night, taking him forcibly out of his bed, and.., dragged him for more than 300 yards down an avenue, and when he finds that one of his accomplices, not so hardened as himself, offered to lend the aggrieved party a beast, in order that he may be enabled to seek a shelter for the night, he heartlessly exclaims, "let the old rascal go and find a shelter where he can".

Miller attempted to justify his conduct by bringing a friend, said to be an attorney, to say that he had recommended him to retain possession of Epsom at all hazards. What is astonishing is that Sir Joshua felt himself bound to state, as an act of justice to the character of Miller that he would not have taken the steps he did, had he not acted under legal advice.

Is not Mr. Miller a magistrate, and ought he not to have known that he was trampling upon the laws of his country when he proceeded to acts of violence to forcibly eject Mr. Reid from Epsom?

Mr. Miller as a magistrate has violently outraged the laws of his country, and justice demands that as a magistrate, he ought to be punished to the law's extent."

On Wednesday November 8th, the case was called again at the Cornwall Assize Court, with Sir Joshua Rowe presiding. To cut a long story short; what then was the fate of Epsom?

It was agreed that Epsom should be put up for sale at public auction, and sold to the highest bidder, the proceeds going to the heirs of Neil.

At the public auction Paul Doig, who had recently returned from Canada, offered one thousand three hundred and fifteen pounds for Epsom. This was the highest bid, and Paul was declared the purchaser. The land was conveyed to him on April 26th, 1838, a little over three months before Emancipation.

Five months later, on September 25, 1838, Paul entered into an agreement with William Tharpe in connection with Epsom Pen. He conveyed Epsom to Tharpe to be held in trust for Mary's "uses and benefits."

What emerges from the struggle for Epsom Pen was not only the tenacity of Thomas (the maverick of the house of Reid) and Mary (father and daughter) but the strong bond that existed between them, which created an unyielding force against the very influential William Miller.

The sight of those two, Thomas and his resolute quadroon daughter, Mary, arm in arm at the trial, created much excited comments among the citizenry.

Thomas died at the age of 92 and was buried at Good Hope.

Mary became the maternal great-great-grandmother of the remarkable Phillip Morrison Fitz -Ritson, who is written about later in this book.

# A FIERY EDITOR

One of the things that enriched Falmouth life was a newspaper called the *Falmouth Post and General Advertiser* (commonly called the *Falmouth Post*). Started in 1835, it was published weekly. The owner and editor was John Castello "the Thunderer of the North". The subscription rate was three pounds per annum, or four pounds when sent by mail. In May 1838, the paper was enlarged, and a portion of its columns was dedicated to literary subjects.

Castello was a hard-hitting editor, striking out at almost everything that seemed in need of correction. His clash with the military shortly after the paper was enlarged, illustrates not only his zeal for law and order, but also the very disorderly behaviour that could sometimes prevail in Falmouth.

One night, Castello observed a group of wild-spirited young officers of Her Majesty's Eighth Regiment engaged in disturbing the peace, shouting and rapping loudly on the doors and windows of people who had gone to sleep. Castello wrote a stern piece criticizing their behaviour. Not long after, he was returning home from a funeral when he noticed some young officers of the regiment assembled near his home. He entered his house and after a while, took a seat at a window. Two of the officers, Ensign Ernest Lavie and Mallet, strolled up. Mallet raised his head, looked at Castello and said:

"Is that the fellow who writes against the officers of the Eighth Regiment?"

Castello didn't answer. Mallet repeated the question and Castello finally said:-

"Yes – what have you to say to me?"

Lavie and Mallet then began to use "the most filthy and obscene language and threatened to inflict a grievous bodily harm" on Castello if he dared to come down. Castello took the matter to court. Ensign Lavie was charged, on Saturday, June 2, with using "vulgar, obscene and threatening language". Lavie admitted that, in a state of excitement, he had used foul language because of the article appearing in the *Falmouth Post* about himself and a brother officer. He was sentenced to pay a fine of twenty shillings, and enter into security to keep the peace for six months.

Castello left the court and was on his way to his office when he was suddenly attacked by two other officers of the Eighth Regiment. They were Sydney Plunkett and Dr. Alexander Douglas Taylor, who was officiating as a medical man in the Regiment. Both were armed with bludgeons. Plunkett struck first, and while Castello was defending himself, Taylor stepped in and hit him. Both men continued to beat the Editor until, from loss of blood, he fell to the ground and was taken into Mr. Kidd's store. No one had come to his help while he was being beaten, but Special Justice Price, coming up at the last moment, took Plunkett and Taylor into custody and went with them to the court house.

A Bench of magistrates was immediately formed, and after Castello's wounds had been dressed, an examination of the events took place. Plunkett and Taylor were bound over to be tried at the next Cornwall Assizes. Castello vowed to leave no stone unturned to get satisfaction."

Castello's rival (his "Lilliputian contemporary") the Editor of the *Standard* newspaper in Montego Bay, wrote jubilantly of Castello's beating and promised him a similar "drubbing" if he should go to Montego Bay to attend the Cornwall Assizes, at which Plunkett and Taylor were to be tried. On June 13, Castello replied in the *Post*, that the Standard's Editor had no great cause to exult, for he himself had recently been harshly dealt with by a gentleman he had slandered "most villainously" in his paper of June 9. Castello said that he, at least, had put up a battle against two men armed with clubs, with no one to help him; but the Standard's Editor (his "pop-gun" adversary), in the presence of his best friends and supporters, had not made the slightest attempt to even wipe off the saliva with which his attacker "so plentifully bespattered him".

At the Cornwall Assizes held in Montego Bay in July, Plunkett and Taylor, "against whom a True Bill had been found by the Grand Jury," for an assault on the Editor of the *Falmouth Post*, appeared in court "and traversed."

When the House of Assembly was dissolved in 1838, a campaign was launched to elect members to the new house. Castello wrote a scorching article exhorting the voters to reject twenty-five members of the old House, whom he referred to as a clique of "ancient oppressors." At the request of Trelawny's reactionary Custos, William Frater, Castello was arrested for sedition. He was bound over to appear and answer the charge at the Cornwall Court. The Attorney-General pronounced the article to be "libellous and calculated to bring the Colonial legislatures of Jamaica and other islands into the contempt and hatred of her Majesty's subjects." The case was submitted to the Colonial Office, and before the appointed day of the trial, the Governor, Sir Lionel Smith (who was disliked by the Legislators but strongly supported by Castello), received a dispatch from Lord Glenelg, the Colonial Secretary, instructing that "the proceedings against Castello be discontinued".

Custos Frater was described by William Knibb, as "a dogged adherent to the system of slavery," who obstinately fought against the plans for the improvement of the emancipated people, which the British government was putting into place. Frater had "opposed to the last" the introduction and passing of the Emancipation Bill, and had "gloried" in his opposition.

In spite of Castello's appeal to the voters, the great majority of the old members were returned to the House. Frater himself won in Trelawny over Castello's favourite, Richard Hill. The outcome was not surprising, for only a tiny fraction of the Jamaican population was eligible to vote.

Castello referred to himself as one of the advocates of "unconditional freedom." He described his newspaper as "an open and avowed supporter" of those liberating measures which the Legislature of Jamaica was resisting, an exposer of fraud and oppression, and a despiser of miscreants. However, after the end of the apprenticeship period in 1838, and with the death of his chief political antagonist in 1839, Custos William Frater, Castello made a startling switch.

It seemed that his notion of freedom for the people, was satisfied with the severing of all legal control of the ex-slaves by their former owners. In 1840, celebrating the anniversary of the termination of apprenticeship, he wrote:

> *Where is now your guard-keeping, where are your Militia General Orders? Where are the secret injunctions given to militiamen to hold themselves in readiness at a moment's warning? All gone! Fled as the last embers of slavery were extinguished.*

Castello expected that the emancipated people would "behave" themselves, and peacefully submit to the needs of their "betters." He seemed content that they should be left where they were: at the bottom of the social ladder, as a pool of convenient labour. That was how most of the "better-off" inhabitants of the island appeared to feel. But the Baptists, led by missionaries like William Knibb and Abbott, were determined that the society should open up areas of opportunity at once for the freed people. They felt that the people had a right to aspire to any level of the society if they had the capabilities.

Castello (who was an Anglican) clashed with Baptist leaders, over their agitation against some newly-passed laws which had the potential to be oppressive. The Baptists also criticized the law requiring Non-Conformists to give economic support to the established (Anglican) church, and insisted that black men be allowed to become magistrates.

Castello entered a crowded meeting in the Falmouth Baptist Church on April 22, 1840. On the platform were Revs. Clark (from Brown's Town), Dexter (Stewart Town), Dendy (Bethephil), Francis (Lucea), Dutten and Ward. Also seated there, were several carpenters and labourers, including Richard Brown, John White and John Dixon. The Chairman was Rev. T.F. Abbott of St. Ann, who had been arrested with William Knibb during the Sam Sharpe Rebellion.

Castello took a seat in one of the front pews of the gallery. Abbott read a statement which had greatly offended the Baptists. It was written by the Governor, Sir Charles Metcalfe, to the Colonial Office on October 16, 1839. The statement severely criticized the labouring population and the Baptist missionaries. Abbott then called on Rev. Benjamin Bull Dexter to move the first resolution.

Dexter was of the view that critics would say the meeting was political, but he didn't think it was wrong for Ministers of the Gospel to interfere in politics when the people were oppressed. The oppressor had predicted that when freedom came, the people would squat down in idleness; cane fields would go to ruin, coffee would be destroyed, estate buildings would be burnt down; but none of these things had happened. The people were industrious, cheerful and glad to earn money from their labour. Only those who wanted to deprive them of their rights were unhappy.

"The more equal the rights and privileges enjoyed by the people, the more will be the prosperity, happiness and tranquility of the country," said Dexter.

In seconding Dexter's resolution, Rev. John Clark said the Governor had been unjust in calling them political partisans. "When bad laws are passed," said Clark, "we must try to get rid of them." The Governor had said they intended to influence the elections, and they certainly would do so.

Clark said he hoped the people would stop supporting the Established Church.

> *We are called upon to pay taxes and support those who cared nothing for the souls of the people. Did they preach to you, teach you to read? They have sent more souls to hell than they have saved.*

Castello leapt to his feet at this point, and interrupted Clark. He said he was an Anglican and would never allow such language to be used in his presence without expressing his indignation. There was a terrible uproar.

*"Turn him out. Throw him out of the window. Throw him over the gallery."*

Shouting as loud as he could, Castello said he would speak regardless of consequences.

Clark repeated the words he had previously used:-

*"The Ministers of the Established Church have sent more souls to hell than they ever saved."*

"That's a lie," Castello yelled.

The whole chapel became a scene of utmost confusion. People rushed towards Castello. Snatching up a pen knife which he used to sharpen his pencil, Castello opened a large blade and shouted:-

*"I will stab the first man to the heart who dares to put his hand upon me."*

The noise was frightful, but Chairman Abbott at last succeeded in restoring order. Clark began to speak once more, continuing his attack on the Established Church.

> "They allowed you to remain in darkness, they left your souls to perish...I sincerely trust that it will not be too long before we do away with the State Church altogether."

As Castello rose to speak, Abbott asked for order, and requested Castello to confine his remarks to the point to which he had taken objection. Castello said:

> "I stand here to express my indignation at the language used against a respectable body of clergymen. He who preaches such doctrines will himself send more souls to hell than all his brother missionaries will save."

Castello's words provoked another great uproar. People rushed towards him. One man was almost upon Castello when he again raised his knife and repeated his threat:

> "I will stab the first person who assaults me.
>
> I care not for your threats. I only regret that other members of the Established Church are not here today to follow my example."

Uproar again. When it subsided Castello sat down.

More resolutions were moved and seconded. The Baptists wanted to know how Governor Metcalfe had reached his conclusions about them, only twenty days after his arrival. He had not even seen a Baptist missionary. Who had advised him? They thought the best thing would be to send Metcalfe away.

Later, when Castello wrote the editorial for his newspaper, he said:-

> The time has arrived when everyone who values his life and property, who desires the peace and happiness of society, who would prevent the island from again being subject to the torch of the rebel (and every horror that follows in the train of rebellion), should arouse himself, and with all the talent that God has endowed him, endeavour to frustrate the evil designs of those persons who are now

*distracting the country with violent and unnecessary agitation.*

*The Baptist missionaries are endeavouring to drive the peasantry into open rebellion, and if their pernicious and unchristian advice remains much longer unnoticed...the estates will be burnt down, our towns will perhaps share the same fate, and hundreds of lives will be sacrificed by an infuriated and misguided mobocracy...*

*People of Jamaica you stand on the brink of a precipice...The labouring population is an ignorant one, easily led away by those in whom they confide. Their minds are already disturbed. They are prepared to follow the instructions of their evil counsellors. The worst passions of mankind are already kindled in their bosoms, and unless prompt measures are taken by the Governor and Her Majesty's Attorney-General, we firmly believe that many months will not pass away, 'ere the standard of Rebellion is unfurled.*

Castello's editorial makes it quite clear that the crisis, which started in 1831 with Sam Sharpe's Rebellion, had not yet passed away. The rebellion, which Castello predicted, would not come until 1865, 25 years later.

## OTHER NEWSPAPERS

According to Dan O'Gilvie, the first newspaper published in Falmouth was the *Cornwall Courier*, in the year 1780. In 1814, the *Cornwall Gazette* and the *Cornwall Chronicle* were operating contemporaneously. John Castello's *Falmouth Post* (with various alterations of the name) came along in 1835. In 1840, it was said that :

> *Falmouth boasts of two printing presses which furnish the reading public with two or more sheets weekly. That of the* Cornwall Courier, *edited by Mr. Dyer, has been most ably conducted by this gentleman for many years, and is considered to be the most consistent journal throughout the island.*

The monthly *Baptist Herald*, with its emphasis on religious subjects, apparently originated in Falmouth. In about 1880, a Printer named John Henry started a weekly paper called the *Falmouth Gazette*, which ran until about 1898. Mr. Henry died in about 1902. There was also the *Trelawny and Public Advertiser* (1874) and the *Trelawny Advance* (1917).

## **LIVELY TIMES**

In 1835, the *Falmouth Post* newspaper reported on December 30 that:-
*The Christmas holidays have passed off with the most perfect harmony. The Cage has not had a solitary inmate in it for some time past. The Specials, Clerk of the Peace and Constables all declare they have nothing to do. Last Sunday was most religiously observed, by free and apprentice, and the churches and chapels of every denomination were crowded, we could almost say, to suffocating; and as far as our information reaches, all went cheerfully to work on Monday.*

A few years later however, it seemed that excitement and rowdy times were back again. In 1837, the *Falmouth Post*, reporting on the events of Election Day said:
*So interesting a day as the 23$^{rd}$ of September has been seldom known in Falmouth. The eagerness of the friends of the respective candidates, the electioneering squibs, the jokes passed on the occasion, the roaring of cannon at each 'plumper' vote, given from a sloop very appropriately named the 'Good Hope,' (belonging to that prince of fellows, Benjamin Harris), the waving banners displayed at several stores, the pleasing countenances of gentlemen's servants, whose hats were decorated with blue cockades, added to the joy manifested by the market people.*

Coming to town in March of that year was a magician Signor Abbondia. On Wednesday, March 29, he presented:-

> *A noble, grand and extraordinary exhibition of wonders of Nature and Art, Scientific and amusing Egyptian Soirees. The band of the 37th Regiment supplied the music, including the Great Overture of Semerade.*
>
> *Divers and astonishing,... Wonderful experiments (including) the play of the Snuff Box, the Candle of Knowledge, Constellate Jewels, The Invisible Pass, The Magical Box, The Fly of Handkerchiefs, The Obedient Carabine that by command will shoot by itself.*
>
> *Abbondio will play the favourite French Air: Le Petit Tambour, arranged as rondo for the flute. Entertainment will conclude with SATAN or the Infernal Chest, one of the best inventions in Mechanism and Legerdemain that human nature can think of. Satan will rise from a locked chest surrounded with fire, and afterwards disappear immediately without the audience discovering wither he has vanished.*
>
> *Admission price six shillings and eight pence. Children under ten, half price.*

The presence of "nude bathers" in the vicinity of the Martha Brae water wheel was a serious problem for respectable citizens. In May, 1837, the *Falmouth Post* reported that:-

> *Several persons are in the habit of bathing themselves near the dam on the Martha Brae River.*
>
> *A gentleman was taking an airing, a few evenings past, accompanied by the female portion of his family. On coming in sight of the water works, he observed upwards of a dozen men in the river, and fortunately stopped his horses in time enough to prevent the ladies from being witnesses of the indecent exposure. We regret that he did not learn the names of the parties, and bring them up to answer the offence before a bench of magistrates.*
>
> *We would suggest that an additional salary be granted to the Constable at Martha Brae, to hire a proper person to attend constantly near the wheel, and prevent a pack of idlers from committing so great an outrage on decency, as the one to which we have alluded.*

As the town grew and the water company had to make extensions to the main pipes, the water supply became unreliable, especially during dry weather when there was not enough water power to turn the *Persian Wheel*. Dry areas like Duncans and its environs, suffered acutely from lack of water, but it wasn't until the 1900s that agitation brought the Dornoch Water Scheme into being.

On the more scandalous side, it was noted that disgraceful practices were being carried on at the race course during, before and after the races. Hundreds of idle "male vagabonds and abandoned women" were in the habit of spending their nights there "and indulging in the most dissolute and sinful pleasures. A nuisance like this (said the *Post*) ought to be immediately put down by the strong arm of the law." The writer hastened to add that his remarks only applied to the town people: "the peasants in the country are seldom seen participating in such demoralizing enjoyments".

In July 1840, several persons were arrested for riding furiously through the streets. A number of false measures were also detected and seized in the market square. They were apparently of the imperial size, and on examination were found to have false bottoms, resulting in buyers receiving about two-thirds of what they were entitled to. The measures were sent to the House of Corrections to be used by the prisoners, but the offenders were not prosecuted "as they promised faithfully to deal more honestly in the future".

On the same day the police, assisted by prisoners from the House of Corrections, rounded up and removed from the streets a great number of hogs, pigs and goats, whose owners allowed them to ramble about and forage for themselves.

One of the most popular places for entertaining was Miss Campbell's lodging house on Duke Street. On Friday, September 24, 1852, several of the bachelors of Trelawny entertained a selected number of ladies at a Quadrille party at Miss Campbell's. Dancing commenced at 9 p.m., and was kept up with great spirit until the next morning."

The bachelors were so pleased, at how well the party came off, that they contemplated giving quarterly entertainments "to their fairer friends and acquaintances," in order to relieve in some measure, the dull monotony for which the town is "unenviably distinguished".

On a Saturday evening, also in September, 1852, a large number of people, including several respectable families, gathered at the Grass Piece near the town to witness a cricket match between the officers of the garrison in Falmouth, and gentlemen of the town and country. The Trelawny gentlemen were unable to get their second innings however because the light failed. The newspaper reported that:

> *At the conclusion of the evening's sport, the players repaired to Miss Campbell's lodging house, where they sat down to an excellent dinner provided for the occasion.*

Plans were made to finish the game the following Saturday but rain washed it out. Undaunted, the Trelawny gentlemen challenged the officers of the garrison stationed at Maroon Town to a match. The officers gave them a "serious drubbing". But at the return match, held at the Grass Piece, the Trelawny players came out on top.

Entertainment was organized to celebrate the occasion, and where else should it be held but at that very popular place, Miss Campbell's lodging house on Duke Street. Mr. Child, the photographer, took advantage of the popularity of Miss Campbell's place, by setting up a temporary studio there. He put an advertisement in the newspaper on October 29, 1852, inviting the public to have photographic portraits taken at Miss Campbell's lodgings. The cost was ten or fifteen shillings for a single portrait, depending on the size. A couple of years later, Mr. Child added a slogan to his advertisement, which said: "Secure the shadow 'ere the substance fades".

The periodic crab hunting expeditions received special attention in 1857. In June of that year, a large number of idlers assembled at night on the outskirts of the town, and on the roads leading to Salt Marsh and Martha Brae, to catch white crabs which were running. They carried lighted torches made of pitch-pine chips, and up until ten o'clock, the roads appeared to be in a blaze of fire.

The crabs were readily sold, but people were warned to be careful, as the crab season was attended by the spread of diarrhoea, having all the "premonitory symptoms" of cholera.

Apparently, a large number of crabs had been caught in the cholera burying ground, which had been filled with dead bodies during the 1851 epidemic, and had been left unfenced.

## **Music, Drama and Funny Advertisements**

Falmouth citizens were amazed at the performance of Signor Pizzini at the Court House on a Saturday night in February, 1859. In playing the violin, "he throws about his body in every possible position, at the same time sustaining his music, and keeping the most perfect time, as if the violin had never left its natural place. His feats of dancing, in all of which he is his own musician are of the most extraordinary character".

The members of the Trelawny Amateur Philharmonic Society gave their first concert in aid of the Volunteers Fund of the parish, on September 17, 1864, in the Court House. It was a decided success.

"We never believed that our town could muster together such a display of musical talent," said the report. "The seats were all taken up and many people had to stand."

In January, February and May 1867, the Trelawny Dramatic Society put on their third, fourth and fifth offerings of plays at the Court House. The plays included the farces: *Raising the Wind, Woodcock's Little Game, Box and Cox,* and

*Little Toddlekins;* the tragedy *Douglas* in five acts, John Tobin's "celebrated and interesting comedy" *The Honeymoon,* and another farce: *Lend Me Five Shillings,* by J. Maddison Morton.

Among the things of interest appearing in the *Falmouth Post* were certain bizarre advertisements. A.J.C. DeLeon, a businessman, who, on removing to a new location in 1858, advised the public that:-

*A.J.C. DeLeon has removed from Market Square to No.17 Market Street, to be known and designated the:*

OLD OAK TREE

*Where he hopes, with the blessing of Divine Providence, his own exertions, the assistance of the influential portion of the community, and the support of his former, and to be hoped-for (under the circumstances of his late heavy losses) new customers, soon to be, as "Richard" said-"himself again."*

*You all did love me once -- not without cause; What cause can withhold you then to support me?*

*Fear not! Rise; follow your leader, and fear no change. Remember "Old Massa" is to be found at the sign of the OLD OAK TREE.*

*Where you will be sure to get good Goods at reasonable prices, with kind treatment, and FAIR PLAY.*

*"Do unto others as you would others do unto you," is the old man's motto.*

*Deal justly and fear not, for God will uphold you."*

Another unusual advertisement came from Theodore Nunes, headed "Death from Joy," in January 1860:-

*It has been currently reported that several persons of high social position as well as thousands of the middle and lower classes, have nearly expired under the excitement produced by the joyful information that Theodore Nunes had opened a Dry Goods and Fancy Establishment in the Falmouth Market Square.*

*The proprietor here begs that they will not think of dying, but get plenty of cash for the purpose of Buying.*

The proprietor of the Alhambra advertised "Cheap Meals".

> Soups for the Working Men of Falmouth at three pence per basin.
> From 11 a.m. until 3 p.m; **Every Day**.

As Christmas approached, the Alhambra advertised that it would be having "Christmas Cheer":

> The above place will be opened all night for callers, and HOT EGG PUNCH will be dispersed to the Customers free.
> Grand illumination on Christmas and New Year's Eve. Call and See.

Electoral statistics in 1859 revealed that 140 persons were registered on the voting list of Trelawny. There were 109 in St. James, 105 in Hanover and 155 in St. Catherine.

A census of Trelawny taken in the 1860s showed a very large proportion of females, especially of those who were unmarried. Women out-numbered men by more than three to two.

# **Gambling**

In 1857, gambling had become so rampant in Trelawny that the newspapers condemned it in the strongest terms. Dr Lewis Ashenheim, who had come to Jamaica in 1843 and moved from Kingston to Falmouth in 1850, gave a lecture on gambling at the Court House on Tuesday, October 6, 1857.

The *Falmouth Post* said it earnestly hoped that "the inhabitants of Falmouth will avail themselves of the opportunity of obtaining an instructive moral lesson on a subject which has been denounced as a vice, so prevalent and so destructive of moral principles, that many…have fallen victims within its pernicious and captivating snare." The Press hoped that the legislature would "enact some stringent law," to quickly correct "this heinous sin."

The morning *Journal of Kingston* said that in Trelawny, gaming was carried to a criminal extent, both among the lower classes, and among people "whose education and position in society ought to deter them." The lower classes of Falmouth and Montego Bay indulge even on Sunday, all about the suburbs…when cards and dice-box are the objects of their devotion from morning till night."

In the village of Pimento Walk near Duncans, gambling was carried on daily, not only for money, but for poultry, bread-kind, etc.

Gaming houses were kept in Falmouth and Martha Brae by notorious swindlers, who robbed the peasantry of their wages. *The Post* said that, among those of higher positions in society "we have heard of large sums of money being lost and won by young men, who are (in) receipt of small incomes".

*The Post* had a problem, however, for while vigorously denouncing gambling, it carried lengthy advertisements promoting the Trelawny Races, the size of the purses, etc.

## **Horse Racing**

Horse racing was one of the biggest attractions in Trelawny. In February 1794, a race course was constructed at Cave Island in the shape of a "complete circle". It was eight furlongs in circumference. Sometimes, there were three days of continuous racing, which attracted crowds from neighbouring parishes. The first Jamaican derby was said to have been run on the Cave Island track, but this is in dispute.

The annual Trelawny races were the high point of social life for many years. On Friday, February 24, 1854, a newspaper reporter said:-

*Never in the recollection of the oldest inhabitant of Trelawny, was so much interest ever manifested by the lovers of the turf, as is exhibited at the present season. The studs of horses...are unprecedented, both numerically and in their high mettle and general racing qualities. We are informed that there are no fewer than fifty horses now in Falmouth, to compete for the purses.*

*For the last fortnight, the course has been attended at an early hour every morning by persons of all classes from the town and country, to witness the trial heats of the noble animals which have been brought from every part of the island. Nothing is now talked of but the races...*

*The usual concomitants (vice and Sabbath desecration) have distinguished the conduct of the lower orders at the race course, where booths have been erected for many weeks past.*

One of the season's race days was vividly described:-

*From early morning hordes of people were to be seen, hastening to the course.*

> *At about ten, the main road was literally thronged with people. Every description of horse-kind, and every possible variety of locomotive machinery, were brought into service: Phaetons, Landaus, Gigs, Dog-carts and Mule-carts (converted into a species of charabanc) were packed with anxious spectators, all attired in the pink of fashion, hastening to witness the sport.*
>
> *The people behaved with great decorum, with the exception of an unfortunate fracas, which induced an indiscreet policeman to strike a respectable-looking person with his baton on the head.*

Five years later, in 1859, the description was just as colourful. For weeks before the races, "turf horses" from outside parishes began arriving in the town, "full of energy and fire". On race day, the trains of carriages of all sorts, saddle horses and numerous crowds of visitors from sister parishes, were more than could be calculated. Booths, tents and other accommodations were erected for the convenience of all parties.

The Grandstand opposite to the Judge's chair was occupied mostly by ladies "wives, mothers, daughters, aunts, cousins, who were entertained at intervals by a small band of musicians. There was a complete cessation of trade and business in Falmouth. Every store, provision shop, drug establishment and even rum shop was closed, as if by concerted and mutual consent."

Early in April, 1864, Falmouth was again filled with visitors who had come to attend the races. There were "ladies of all styles of beauty, dressed in costly silks and satins," and as they passed, "lounging in splendid carriages that are drawn by high-mettled horses, we gaze admiringly at the dimpled, rosy cheeks & sparkling eyes of the young; and respectfully at the full, matronly developments of the dear mamas and aunts".

The ladies were accompanied by a large number of "Lords of the Creation; among them" Merchants and Planters, Lawyers and Doctors, Bankers, Officers and Customs, Collectors of Dues, Editors of newspapers, of three of the thirteen Patriots who refused to do business with His Excellency the Lieutenant-Governor (Edward John Eyre).

> *There was an immense assemblage of persons at the Course. Keepers of Booths effected profitable sales of Champagne, Madeira, Sherry, Port; liqueurs, Punch-Royal and Punch Plebian; besides Brandy, Gin and native 'Stiggins.' Tables were abundantly supplied with eatables of every description, including cakes, jams, jellies and luscious fruits; and in the small 'shanties' were eatables and drinkables also for 'the Million.' The Sports terminated late in the evening and were succeeded by costly dinner parties, musical soiree and balls, all of which were fashionably attended.*

The Mule Race was won by a man named Blackall.

In 1865, however, (the year of the Morant Bay Rebellion), an air of depression seemed to have settled over everything, not only in Trelawny but in other parts of the island. It was reported on Friday, March 17, that there was very little excitement over the Trelawny Races. This, said the writer, was because of the "dullness of the times", which prevented many from attending the race course. Only two of three places of business were closed, and few visitors came from Kingston, St. Ann, St. James and other parishes. The whole affair was so tame that fears were expressed that there might be little if any effort to get up a meeting for 1866, especially as the Legislature would not be granting the next Queen's Purse (the Premier Race) to Trelawny.

When the races began on the 14th, there were only about twenty carriages on the course. The Grand Booth was poorly patronized. Only about thirty seats were occupied by the ladies. The sale of refreshments was small and booth keepers complained of losses. Their old customers complained, on their part, of the lack of money to spend. In April, the treasurer of the races was unable to meet all the claims sent to him, because of the non-payment of sums subscribed towards the races.

# DANGEROUS AND AMAZING THINGS

At three o' clock on the morning of Friday, November 26, 1852, people in almost all the houses in Falmouth were awakened by one of the most severe earthquakes ever felt in the town. It lasted for about twenty-five seconds, with "undulations from north to south."

Over twelve years later, on the night of Wednesday, February 15, 1865, a very severe earthquake was felt in the town at ten minutes after seven. Many of the inhabitants rushed terror-stricken into the streets.

In November, 1852, a party of soldiers marched through the town, preceded by drummers and fifers. They were trying to get recruits for the Third West India Regiment and were successful in getting "one or two Africans to enlist". These Africans were apparently part of a group that had recently migrated to Jamaica as workers, at the expense of the government.

The *Falmouth Post* was unhappy at what took place. It wanted the authorities to bring to the attention of the Commander of the Forces (General Bunbury) the possible danger to the agricultural community, " if immigrants imported at a considerable expense, are prevailed upon to enter the army, and abandon the employment for which they are required."

Six years later (1858), displaying a bit of racial contempt, *The Post* drew attention to the new military uniform of the West India regiments:

> *The Black Regiments of soldiers, at present in the island, are now wearing a costume similar to that of the Zouaves who served in the Crimean War. It consists of a white flannel jacket, a pair of large, blue breeches, made after the fashion of petticoat trousers used by sailors of the olden time, a light-red cap and Blucher-boots. No stockings, no gaiters, no leather collar-round the neck; and quashie seems quite happy at being relieved of old encumbrances. The dress is peculiarly adapted to his habits, and becomes him well.*

Added to the list of amazing things was a "red glare in the heavens, extending from the horizon, half way over the town of Falmouth", which appeared between the hours of twelve and one o' clock on Friday morning September 2, 1859. People living in the country that saw it, thought that Falmouth was on fire. "The sight was grand but terrifying."

A newspaper article in 1863 said that for the last eight or ten years, the mango crop had failed in several parts of the parish. Thousands of large, healthy trees that formerly were prolific, ceased to bear; occasionally, some put out blossoms, but these soon withered. No one was able to say what caused the problem.

A breed of pigs that had been accustomed to a diet which included mangoes, seriously declined. Consequently, the "savory young pork", which took second place to no other in the world, had very much diminished.

In June 1865, one James Miller from Duncans, was sentenced to two months at hard labour for stealing four mangoes from Holland Estate. Miller said he had gone there to look for work, but was not successful. Becoming hungry, he had helped himself to the mangoes.

At about 7:00 p.m. on Monday, September 23, 1867, the towns-people were alarmed by a tremendous crash which came from the direction of the Parish Church. When they hurried there, they found that the rope, by which the striking weight of the clock had been suspended, had broken. The 500 lb weight had fallen 84 feet (sic) to the ground and destroyed a portion of the ceiling. Only an hour or so earlier, the Rector had been at the Church conducting a funeral. The Church was described at the time as being in a most shameful and dilapidated condition.

On Friday, October 25, 1867, between twenty and thirty soldiers of the Third West India Regiment went on a rampage. Armed with huge sticks, to the ends of which razors were tied, they rushed from their barracks through the street, attacked everyone in their path, including policemen, and smashed the windows in a shop called the People's House, run by Desouza and Lazarus.

Captain Hewett of the regiment rode up but was unable to control them. They turned on Lieutenant Alman, one of their officers, and struck him. Hewett eventually managed to get them back into the barracks, and several were subsequently tried at the Police Court. One reason given for the disturbance was that the soldiers felt they had been cheated in a shooting match between the police and themselves, which had taken place the previous day. The Custos had awarded the Silver Cup to Sergeant-Major Hinds of the Constabulary.

A petition was signed in 1868, requesting that Market Square be improved by the removal of the Old Cage, which had been erected over 60 years earlier to house disorderly persons. The Cage was being used to lock up prisoners at night, "who, by the disgraceful noise they make, disturb the inhabitants residing in the vicinity". It was suggested that the lock-up in the lower part of the Court House be used instead, to confine prisoners who were apprehended during the night.

1870 was the year when Falmouth registered its first case of "Breach of Promise of Marriage". John Atterbury and Janet Hill were engaged for seven years, during which she bore him a child. No wedding was forthcoming so Janet's mother raised the devil with John and got him to promise to marry Janet.

John continued to visit Janet. She became pregnant for him again, but when the demand for marriage was once more raised, John refused.

Janet and her mother took him to the Falmouth District Court, with Philpotts Brown appearing for the plaintiff and R.W. Swan for the defendant. The spectators were very much amused by the case, and it created a good deal of laughter. In the end, the Judge (Hon. Harry Davidson), found for the plaintiff: twenty-one pounds plus costs.

## Big Food

Two sugar canes, measuring eighteen feet each, were sent to the office of the *Falmouth Post* in 1837. They came from the garden of Mr. R.G. Murray.

Three years later, on April 1, 1840, a pumpkin weighing seventy pounds was sold to the mess-man of the 68th Regiment in the town. "It grew on Springfield Pen, the property of James Gerrard. Another from the same place weighed forty-five pounds, measuring five feet in circumference."

On Tuesday, May 4, 1852, a fisherman named Taylor caught two large June fish at Long Bay. The first measured six-feet in length, two feet four inches around the body, and weighed two hundred and sixty-five pounds. The second weighed eighty-five pounds and was four feet in length.

Both June fish were put up for sale at a stall in Market Square. They were quickly bought at six-pence per pound.

In September, Albert Haughton landed a June fish, which weighed one hundred and fifty-four lbs. Some portions were sold at nine pence per pound. A large quantity remained unsold however, and at a late hour, was offered for three pence per lb. But no purchasers could be had.

On the morning of February 21, 1869, Frederick Edwards, bettered Taylor's record; he picked up a giant June fish he saw floating in the Falmouth harbour, which measured 7 feet long by 5 feet in circumferences. It weighed three hundred lbs and was not quite dead. Nobody would buy any of it, so the "monster of the deep was cut up and corned".

In June 1874, at Good Hope Estate, then owned by F.R. Coy, there was a large pig weighing over two hundred pounds. The pig had been reared principally on coconuts, "which in our opinion (said the reporter) is equal to any farinaceous food imported for fattening stock".

Four years earlier (in May, 1870), Mr. Coy had reared a hog on Good Hope weighing three hundred and twenty-six pounds, which was five feet from snout to tail, and four feet in circumference. That animal also had been raised primarily on coconuts.

A few weeks earlier (in April, 1870) astonished residents saw a large yam at the store of William Browne. It was seven feet long and weighed nearly seventy pounds, and had been taken from an old provision ground at Magotty Estate. Mr. Browne sent it to England, in the charge of a ship's captain who sailed from Lucea, to be presented to Her Majesty, Queen Victoria.

## Shipwreck

The Barque "Medina", commanded by Captain Tindale, was a frequent visitor to Falmouth. On September 25, 1874, on the way from London to Jamaica, Captain Tindale saw a waterspout about a half mile astern, coming straight for the Medina. He just had time to haul up one side of the foresails before the waterspout struck.

"The great cone of water was whisking round and round overhead; the lower part was close to the stern, the sea flying up and whisking round it, fifteen feet high." The ship's stern was pressed down when the waterspout hit it, and she was thrown over to port. According to Tindale:

> *The great cone of water was terrific, worse than ever I experienced in any hurricane. I was holding on to the bulwarks and was almost forced away by the strength of wind and rush of water.*
>
> *The spout, after passing over the whole length of the ship, went away to port and dispersed. The track of it was well marked by a wake in the water, such as a fast ship would make. Immediately after it passed, we had a Thunderstorm, accompanied by forked lighting and rain.*

A little over a month later, while the Medina was in Falmouth harbour, a storm struck. It came after twenty-four hours of heavy and incessant rain.

As a result of the storm, the northern side of the new Masonic temple was blown down, and the eastern side, which was just being erected, was damaged. A blacksmith's shop on Duke Street was destroyed and various other houses in the town damaged. Many trees were uprooted and thrown across the streets, and many fences knocked down. The Medina's cable snapped and several smaller vessels in the harbour were seriously damaged.

The most amazing thing, however, was when the wreck of a large vessel, the Othello, which had sunk thirty years before in three or four fathoms of water at Rio Bueno, was thrown up "high and dry" on the beach. Her timbers were found to be all sound, and the oaken pins holding the timbers and planks together were all perfectly good, in spite of thirty years under water. The Othello had been loaded with salt, consigned to the late Thomas Tenison, who did business as a merchant in the town.

Dan O'Gilvie in his book, *History of the Parish of Trelawny*, tells the story of the wreck of the barque Fontabelle at Salt Marsh. O'Gilvie says that the ship's captain was John Nicholson, and that the wreck occurred on October 31, 1874, during the hurricane that lasted from October 31 to November 2. Fifteen men lost their lives, including three captains.

However, the records of Trelawny Burials 1871-1883 Vol. 18 indicate that the Fontabelle was wrecked on December 10, 1880, and that her "master" was Edward Nixon, not John Nicholson. O'Gilvie probably mixed up the 1874 and the 1880 storms.

According to O'Gilvie, the 600 ton Fontabelle moved out of Falmouth harbour on October 31 with a cargo of sugar and rum. The ship had spent several weeks in harbour and the crew was well known to the townspeople.

Captain Nicholson's wife was on board, and she had her big Newfoundland dog whose name was Samuel. The sea was calm and the wind light as Fontabelle was towed out to sea by the pilot's boat. Medina and other ships in the harbour saluted as Fontabelle went by. About two miles from shore, the pilot disembarked. The wind had fallen and Fontabelle was motionless.

At noon, there was still no wind, but swells developed in the sea. The ship was tossed about more and more. It began to drift ashore in the direction of Salt Marsh, a village about three miles west of Falmouth. Hoping to stop the drift, Captain Nicholson lowered all the anchors; but a great wind arose and the waves grew stronger, and Fontabelle was driven ever closer to shore.

Captains Roach and Hopewell of the "Blanch" and "Medina" rowed out in their boats to see what help they could give. They rowed three miles, and when they reached Fontabelle offered to take off Mrs. Nicholson; but she refused to leave her husband.

Night fell. Roach and Hopewell returned to their ships, which were also in danger. The wind increased in intensity. Fontabelle dragged her anchors. Her furled sails were ripped. Riggings and spars broke. The anchor chains parted. Finally, the ship was hurled on to the coral rocks. In less than an hour, she was pounded to pieces.

The captain and the crew were flung into the sea, and desperately grabbed at bits of wood and other objects floating by. A Trelawny boy named Henry Jones strapped himself to a spar, and was propelled towards the rocky shore. Mrs. Nicholson was also flung into the water and was struggling to keep afloat. She was on the point of giving up when the Newfoundland dog, Samuel, swam towards her in the darkness and grabbed her hair. Encouraged by Samuel's presence she renewed her efforts and reached the beach, bruised and battered but alive. Henry Jones was also washed alive on to the beach, but his limbs were broken by the rocks and his body severely bruised.

In the morning, people went out to Salt Marsh. They took up Mrs. Nicholson and Henry Jones. Along the beach, they found the battered dead bodies of sailors. Some of their faces were smashed beyond recognition. They also found the dead body of Captain Nicholson.

The bodies were placed in coffins and taken three miles to the Falmouth Parish Church. Hundreds of carriages joined the procession, and just about everybody turned out to witness the mass funeral. Shops were closed. There was much weeping and sobbing. The town remained in mourning for a month, and flags were flown at half-mast.

After weeks of medical attention, amid expressions of genuine sympathy, the distraught Mrs. Nicholson boarded the Medina, and returned to her home and children in Scotland. For years, she wrote to many of the people in Falmouth who had been kind to her during her period of great distress. The story of the wreck of the Fontabelle was one of the chief topics in Falmouth, as people recalled that harrowing event.

The Falmouth Burial Records do not list all the fifteen men who are said to have drowned at Salt Marsh, but they show the three captains who died as a result of the storm:

*John Prince Hopewell, 34, Master of Barque "Medina"; died December 10, 1880, at Salt Marsh. Drowning. Buried December 12, cemetery.

*Edward Nixon, 52, Master of Barque "Fontabelle"; died Dec. 10, 1880, Salt Marsh. Drowning. Buried December 12, cemetery.

*James Woolley, 34, Master of Barque "Dundee." died Dec. 10, 1880, Salt Marsh. Drowning. Buried Dec. 12, cemetery.

Also listed were four of Fontabelle's crew: the cook, A. Hawley, 26; Ordinary Seaman D. Georder, 20; Ordinary Seaman R. Canton, 21 and Ordinary Seaman Charles Murphey, 38.

# **SOCIAL UNREST**

The traditional excitement and fashionable social events, accompanying the annual races, helped to obscure feelings of discontent among a large section of the "ordinary" people. Jamaica had experienced only about twenty years of full freedom, and many important questions were far from settled. There were many civil disturbances and one of the most serious occurred in July and August of 1859. It arose from a dispute about "the Right of Possession", between Theodore Buie, the "coloured" son of the late owner of Florence Hall Penn, and the attorney of the sisters of the said late owner.

The attorney for the sisters (who of course were Theodore Buie's "white" aunts) tried to evict Theodore from Florence Hall Penn, as he alleged that the sisters were the rightful owners. Theodore and his friends and supporters thought otherwise. For nearly three months, the friends and supporters gathered at Florence Hall Penn, day after day, and prevented the attorney from evicting Theodore. He spent a lot of money feeding them. One supporter declared that: "If Theodore Buie is compelled to give up possession of Florence Hall, he should do so without leaving a stick of the building standing".

The Clerk of the Peace and the Magistrates concerned with the case, were accused of being influenced by class and colour prejudice. On Monday, August 1 (the twenty-first anniversary of Full Freedom) hundreds of people assaulted the police while they were trying to serve warrants against the Florence Hall rioters. When the case was being heard in the Circuit Court, presided over by Judge Richard O'Reilley, the proceedings were interrupted by the excited mob, who declared that none of the rioters would be imprisoned regardless of what the jury decided.

Judge O'Reilley stayed the proceedings until police reinforcements could arrive from St. Ann, St. James and Hanover. The rioters were sent back to the jails but they were rescued by the mob. A magistrate and two policemen were wounded in the clash. The windows of the house in which the Superintendent of the prison lived, were smashed with stones. The mob then marched on the police station. Inspector Taafe armed his men and placed them in strategic positions to block the entry of the mob. Nevertheless, the windows of the station were destroyed, and a panel of one of the doors was broken by a heavy stone.

Eight magistrates hurried to the police station and tried in vain to persuade the mob to disperse. Stones were again thrown and a policeman was severely wounded on the forehead. The Riot Act was read and the people were advised again to go quietly to their homes.

They left. The magistrates thought the crisis was over, and most of them went home. But the people, instead of going home, went to the Court House and smashed several panes of glass. Then they headed for the homes of three of the magistrates and broke more windows. They went back to the police station, with the intention of storming it.

Inspector Taafe had ranged his men across the street and two magistrates (Salmon and Abraham) who had remained at the station, tried to calm the mob. Mr. Abraham told the police not to fire unless they received an order to do so. It is said that a pistol was fired from the crowd and stones and bottles were thrown. Justice Salmon gave the order to fire and the policemen let off a volley. Two women fell dead. Several men and women were wounded. A great yell went up from the crowd. They took up the dead and wounded and carried them away. The other justices hurried back to the police station and, with their colleagues, hastily made plans to protect property and life. Special constables, recruited from the "respectable" classes, were sworn in.

At half past eleven, there was a cry of "fire". A building connected to Charles Delgado's drug store had been set ablaze. Mr. Morales and other gentlemen, working together with their servants, managed to contain the blaze. At four in the morning, another fire broke out at one of the stores on the Trelawny wharf which was leased by George DeLisser and Son. A large crowd gathered and the fire was put out in a little over half an hour. A third fire was also started that night.

The justices met at the Court House at 10 a.m. the next day. Dispatches were sent to Governor Eyre reporting what had happened. Police reinforcements came from St. Ann, St James, and later from Hanover. The Circuit Court was closed. In the evening, a cart accompanied by armed policemen, carried the bodies of the two slain women to the church yard. When the party was returning, stones were thrown at them, and Justice Kitchin was struck on the leg.

A party of special constables removed all the guns and bayonets from the Armoury at the Barracks, and took them back to the police station where they were made ready for use. Special constables were placed on guard at the Court House and the streets were patrolled by armed men from nine at night until half-past four in the morning.

On Friday, August 5, the steamer *Wye* brought two companies of the Second West India Regiment to Falmouth. On landing, they marched at once to the Barracks. According to the angry editor of the *Falmouth Post*, the arrival of the troops put an end to the swaggering through the streets of the "unwashed multitude". There was no more resistance to the police in the execution of their duty, no more threats of vengeance accompanied by cries of blood for blood, no more singing of indecent songs by profligate women, no more savage yellings and hootings when the Special Constables went their rounds, no more abusive language when respectable ladies appeared at the windows of their houses. Theodore Buie was captured by a military and police force on Saturday morning, 6 August. He was put in jail. The *Falmouth Post* felt that Jamaica was fortunate to have a Governor like Edward John Eyre:

> We have seldom had at the head of affairs a Governor better qualified to deal promptly and effectually with such a case.

History was to have an entirely different view of Governor Eyre.

Under the headline, LYNCH LAW IN TRELAWNY, the *Falmouth Post* reported that on Wednesday, September 13, 1865, serious breaches of the peace were committed at Marldron in St. James, and Deeside in Trelawny. At the centre of the disturbance was Henry Selvyn Gilbourne of the Trelawny Court, who was Assistant to the Collector of Petty Debts, and Assistant to the Deputy Marshal of Trelawny, M.A. Nunes.

Nunes asked Gilbourne to carry out a Writ of Attachment at the request of John DeLisser and company, against William Downie, shopkeeper of Deeside. When Nunes heard that Downie was fraudulently removing goods and a large sum of money to Marldron, ten miles away from Deeside, he directed Henry Gilbourne to go to Marldron on September 13, while he himself took the Deeside route.

Gilbourne was accompanied by a constable from Falmouth named Theodore Benjamin. As soon as he arrived, he went to the house of Downie's father-in-law where he found a quantity of goods and over seventy pounds in money hidden on the premises. While he was making the levy on them, a noisy crowd gathered. Several persons began throwing goods through the windows, but Gilbourne recovered them. Then a woman ran off with a chest containing the money. Gilbourne gave chase and recovered it.

On the return journey, laden with his levy and guarded by a few district constables, Gilbourne was way-laid on the Deeside road by Downie and over a dozen men. They were armed with huge sticks and clubs, and, in trying to recover the levy, gave Gilbourne a severe beating. With the guard of district constables, Gilbourne managed to stand them off and, though badly roughed-up, reached Falmouth with the levy. Nunes was also abused and set at defiance at Deeside by Downie and his gang of hired ruffians.

*The Post* said it was informed that criminal proceedings were being taken against all those concerned in "setting law and order at defiance"; and was confident that they would receive the punishment they deserved.

Three years after the ambush, Henry Gilbourne was in the news again, when he had a brief brush with a police corporal, who created a disturbance which threw the town into a state of excitement. Henry's family, the Gilbournes, were foundation members of the Falmouth Methodist Church, and Henry involved himself in the various church activities. On Saturday, May 16, 1868, he attended a Methodist (Wesleyan) Bazaar, held in the Ballroom of the Court House.

On duty at the Court House was Corporal Gibson, who was drunk. At about eight o' clock, Gibson ordered three constables to arrest a man who was standing on one of the steps leading to the ballroom. The constables refused to obey the order, because it was clear to them that the man was not committing an offence. Gibson became angry and ordered a corporal named Wakefield to arrest the disobedient constables. Wakefield said he was not on duty, and Gibson became even more infuriated. A noisy argument developed, during which Gibson completely lost control of himself. He abused both Wakefield and the Inspector who appeared on the scene, using the "most vulgar and indecent expressions".

At this stage, Henry Selvyn Gilbourne intervened. In a friendly manner, he advised Corporal Gibson to calm down and keep quiet. Gibson turned on him with "a volley of abuse," calling him a damn fool and a damn brute, etc, etc. The enraged corporal strode into the Constabulary Guard Room, which was in the Court House. He came back with a long, thick club "with which he committed a serious assault on the person of Wakefield".

The situation now became almost hilarious. Under the heavy blows he received from Gibson, Wakefield yelled: "Murder, murder". Instead of coming to his assistance the three constables ran away. Wakefield also fled, hotly pursued by Gibson. In his drunken rage, Gibson chased Wakefield through the streets for a considerable distance, striking with his big stick at anyone who came within his reach.

Not a single policeman appeared to try to put an end to Gibson's violent rush. It was a courageous civilian named Guthrie who finally tripped him and brought him down to the ground. He grabbed the fallen Corporal Gibson and with the assistance of other civilians, dragged him to the police station. There he was handcuffed by Sergeant Major Redwood. In spite of his manacled hands, Gibson struck Redwood on the face with a severe blow.

A large crowd of people had gathered by this time, and Gibson was taken to the Cage in the town square where he was locked up, like any common disturber of the peace. The three constables who had fled were punished by the Inspector, whose name was Mitchell. Gibson himself was sent to headquarters to face the Inspector-General, Major Prendeville. The *Falmouth Post* had no doubt that Prendeville would "severely punish the refractory Corporal for his outrage against the public peace".

# GOVERNOR EYRE'S VISIT TO FALMOUTH

In 1863, *The Post* reported the death of Arthur Dunlop Eyre, infant son of His Excellency, the Lieutenant-Governor Edward John Eyre. Young Eyre died on Saturday, April 4, at Flamstead in St. Andrew, which Eyre used as a country retreat. Shortly after, Eyre's wife sailed for England.

Governor Eyre was described in a newspaper editorial of October 13, 1865, as being peculiarly unfortunate in the policy he adopted for administering the government of Jamaica. "He has not courted Golden Opinions, nor has he made the slightest effort to acquire even a limited amount of popularity. He has cooled friends and heated enemies." Nevertheless, when Eyre visited Trelawny a little over a year earlier, as a stop on his tour of the island, the Gentry and better-off citizens fawned upon him. He was the good Queen's representative, an authentic bit of England in their midst. He was a living embodiment of the mother country which to them was the centre of the world. His coldness and ineptness were set aside; his ability to act decisively against the "out-of-order" multitude was applauded.

Preparations were made for several days before his arrival on Wednesday, July 20, 1864. The streets of the town were repaired and swept, the public and parochial buildings were put in order and, on the morning of his arrival, there was a "lively display" of the flags of all nations at the church, at stores and residences, and on board vessels in the harbour.

An arch decorated with evergreens and flowers was erected at the entrance to the town by Mr. Kidd, the Superintendent of the Prisons. He was assisted by Ministers of the Gospel, Merchants, Planters and other gentlemen, all anxious that there should be a proper manifestation of respect for the representative of their beloved Sovereign. In the centre of the arch was the word WELCOME, in red letters on a white background. British flags flanked the arch. Another arch was erected 50 or 60 yards lower down by a Mrs. Taylor.

The main street was filled with hundreds of people, and at half-past eight, when the Governor's arrival was signaled, "the whole town was thrown into a state of loyal excitement". When Eyre arrived, three hearty cheers were given, and he bowed. "A merry peal was rung on the church bells by a number of respectable young men, a salute was fired in front of the Court House, where the Police under the command of Inspector Mitchell was stationed; and when his Excellency alighted at the residence of Robert Nunes Esq. Junior representative of the Parish, the populace shouted: "Welcome, welcome".

The handsomely-furnished drawing room of Nunes' residence was filled when Eyre was ushered in at half-past nine. Thirty-five gentlemen of rank and high position in Society were present. Eyre seemed astonished at first, but in a few moments "his countenance beamed with joy", and to every individual who was introduced he gave "a friendly English shake of the hand". Breakfast was then served. The table was adorned with vases of flowers. "There was a magnificent display of silver and crystal. Tea and coffee were handed round in richly-painted cups and saucers of pure China, and...the wines were 'first rate' and delightfully cooled." Breakfast lasted until half-past ten.

At half-past eleven the Governor inspected the Trelawny Volunteer Corps, drawn up in full dress on the Parade Ground in front of the Court House, under the command of Captain Frederick Lindo. Eyre then entered the Court House. He was loudly cheered by over two hundred gentlemen on his way to the ballroom where a large number of ladies was assembled. The Trelawny Volunteers, preceded by their band, entered the room. 'God Save the Queen' was played and three cheers given for the Queen and the Royal Family. Addresses were presented by the Custos, Magistrates, Ministers of Religion and others. A presentation ceremony then took place, after which Eyre toured the public offices in the building.

He then left the Court House, got into his carriage and visited the Suspension Bridge (which was being repaired), the Anglican Church, the Wesleyan and Baptist Chapels, the Presbyterian Kirk, the District Prison, Marine Hospital, Poor House, Barracks and Police Station. As he went from place to place, hundreds followed his carriage, including many gentlemen on horseback. After refreshments (again at the house of Robert Nunes), Eyre returned to the Court House at 3 p.m. for a banquet.

The tables were heavily laden. "Everything in the way of fish, flesh and fowl was there," along with confectionary and iced wines. Sixty gentlemen were present. Loyal and patriotic toasts were proposed, and the Governor was given proof that he was "held in esteem by the wealth, respectability and intelligence of Trelawny". The band played an appropriate tune after each speech.

Eyre gave a heartfelt reply, and at 5 p.m., left the Court House for Roslin Castle, residence of the Hon. G. Cunningham. It was said that never had any Governor, "not even Lord Metcalfe at the height of his popularity, been treated with more attention in the town of Falmouth".

*The Post* said that "many a fervent prayer was offered to the Throne of Grace that God's blessing may rest on (Eyre's) labours, and that in his administration of the affairs of the colony, he may receive the co-operation and aid of every individual who desires the well-being of the land".

When the Morant Bay Rebellion broke out in October, 1865, *The Post* came out strongly in support of the harsh measures adopted by Eyre against the "ignorant lower orders", the savage multitude. It rejoiced over the execution of George William Gordon who was seen as the arch fiend. The paper (in the person of its Editor and Publisher) had come a long way from the days when it had fought vigorously against the opponents of freedom. It had become not just conservative, but reactionary. It reflected the sentiments of much of the "wealth and respectability" in Trelawny, who sent an address to Eyre thanking him for the prompt energetic measures he adopted to crush the rebellion.

After the Morant Bay Rebellion, Governor Eyre issued an order that there should be no blowing of horns, shells or other noisy instruments in the public thoroughfares of the island. As a result, Christmas of 1865 was very dull in Falmouth.

On April 16, 1866, it was rumoured in Spanish Town and Falmouth that Governor Eyre had again fallen from his horse, and that he had fractured three of his ribs. He was on his way from Flamstead to Kingston.

Mrs. Eyre returned to Jamaica and gave birth to a child, apparently early in 1866. *The Post* reported the christening of the child in the Spanish Town Cathedral on June 13, 1866. The child "was known in the family circle by the endearing appellation of Rebellion".

On August 18, 1866, the 28 anniversary of Emancipation, Falmouth was very quiet. None of the places of worship were opened for Divine service, and there was not the slightest manifestation of rejoicing. Very few country people came to town and the sales of shopkeepers did not exceed those of any ordinary day in the year.

August 1, 1868 was no better. There was no Divine Service in the town and no rejoicing. A lot of country people were coming in but they bought very little. Perhaps it was the Morant Bay Rebellion still casting its shadow of gloom.

*The Post* complained that the Baptists had taught the country people to be politicians, instead of Christians. In 1866, it reported that several advertisements had appeared in Kingston newspapers, offering sugar estates, penns, dwelling houses and furniture for sale, by persons who intended to leave the island to settle in the United Kingdom or the United States.

"It is said," the article continued, "(that) some of the principal merchants on the south side in Cornwall, are determined to wind up their affairs as quickly as possible, with the view of investing their means in other places, where they consider property will be better protected, and safer, than in Jamaica."

# BRIGHTENING THE DULL TIMES

Following the Morant Bay Rebellion and the abolition of the Constitution, a new Governor was elected to run the newly created Crown colony. He was Sir John Peter Grant who succeeded Eyre. On March 30, 1867, Grant paid a visit to Falmouth but he didn't receive as warm a reception from the town's high society as had Governor Eyre, whom they favoured. It is very likely that Grant was seen as a part of the machinery which had brought about Eyre's disgrace and his near indictment for murder over the death of George William Gordon.

Sir John sanctioned the appropriation of one hundred guineas for the Queen's Purse race, and also gave a Governor's Purse to be contested for. This still did not stop the downward slide of the annual Trelawny races. At the races held on Tuesday, September 8, 1868, there were not more than a score of carriages at the course. The Grandstand was "thinly attended", and the seats occupied by the ladies (one of the premier attractions) were very few. Booth keepers complained of heavy losses as the sales of liquor and refreshments were small. The race reporter said he had never witnessed such a poor display.

Things improved on Christmas Day. The market was very attractive and presented a lively appearance. A large number of people attended, in spite of the sharp, bleaky wind which was blowing and continued throughout the entire day. There were at least 3,000 lbs of beef in the several stalls.

The members of the Falmouth Cricket Club played a match at the Grass Piece on New Year's day (1869), starting at noon. Merchants and other businessmen agreed to close their establishments for the greater part of the day, and a tent was erected for visitors. The contending teams wore red and blue rosettes.

To further enliven the dull times, a public ball was given at the Court House later in the year. Invitations to the ball were issued to a large number of ladies and gentlemen in adjoining parishes.

On the day of the ball (Wednesday, September 29), a large number of persons arrived from Kingston, St. Ann and other parishes. The Ballroom of the Court House was elegantly decorated with flowers of various kinds, and the flags of many nations. The Court Room was prepared as a Supper Room.

The entrance to the building was splendidly illuminated with variegated and other lamps, and there was a blaze of lights in every room. The troops under Captain Grace, and headed by a Drum Corps, marched from the barracks to await Major General Luke Smythe O' Connor (of Morant Bay Rebellion fame) who was the guest of honour. The General along with his entourage and Custos Nunes, arrived at 9:30pm. A gun was fired from the ship "Speedwell" in the harbour and the troops gave a salute.

Dancing commenced at 9:45. Quadrilles, waltzes, lancers, gallops followed each other in rapid succession. At 2:00 a.m., the Supper Room was thrown open for the more than 250 guests. After the sumptuous supper, dancing resumed until 5:00 a.m..

On Wednesday May 24, 1871, the fifty-second anniversary of Queen Victoria's birth was celebrated with enthusiasm in Falmouth. Public offices were closed and there was a general suspension of busines between two and three in the afternoon.

Early in the morning, a gun was fired from the Barque Medina and, immediately after, all the ships in the harbour, including HMS Lapwing, were decorated with flags of every description. At eleven, a detachment of the First West India Regiment under Captain Gibb, turned out in full dress; went through several military evolutions and fired a *feude joie*. At twelve, a Royal Salute was fired from the Medina and Eleanora.

At 1 p.m., Military Athletic Sports were held at the Parade Ground. The events included foot racing, high jump, throwing the cricket ball, hop step and jump, hurdle race, heavy marching order race, wrestling, pipe smoking, sack race, wheel barrow race, water pail race, etc. Guns were fired throughout the day on a piece of open ground in front of the Falmouth District Prison, by Superintendent T.P. Kidd.

There was almost no celebration of the anniversary of Emancipation in August, 1874. However, it was observed that small settlers were daily bringing immense quantities of yams, etc. into Lucea. Many of them were shipping "the abundant products of their industry to Montego Bay, Falmouth, St. Ann's Bay, Kingston and other parts of the island, where high prices can be obtained". *The Falmouth Post* also carried an article from St. Thomas in the East which said that "there can be no doubt that the labouring people are getting everyday more and more independent, and, unfortunately, we are to a great extent entirely dependent on them".

## THE BIG SCANDAL OF 1867

The people of Trelawny and Falmouth in particular, were shocked when news came that James Wilson, Secretary of the Trelawny Savings Bank, had been charged with embezzlement.

Wilson was a Churchwarden, and, on Thursday morning, June 13, he rode to Ulster Spring with Rev. D.R. Littlejohn, Rector of the parish. From Ulster Spring, they went to a place, a short distance from Albert Town, where a new church was being built. They inspected the building then returned to Albert Town, to spend the night in the house of a man named Baker.

The next day Wilson, Baker and two men named Murray and Carter, set out for the backlands of Troy, on the border of the neighbouring parish of Manchester. Wilson was going to collect back rent owing to him by tenants on a property called Wilson's Run. He told Rector Littlejohn he would return that night or early next morning.

Littlejohn sat up late, but when Wilson didn't appear, he went to bed. Soon after midnight he heard horses' hoofbeats in the yard. Going to the window he asked:

"Who is there?"

"Oh, Minister," a voice replied, "we have lost the squire."

The riders in the yard were Murray and Carter. They told Littlejohn they had lost Wilson in the woods from 1p.m. Baker appeared later on to add his version of the story. He said that Wilson and he left their mules at the entrance to the "heavy" woods. They walked for about three miles, and then Wilson complained of feeling tired. He bared one of his arms and asked him to feel the great heat coming from it. Wilson then sat on a damp log but rose in a few minutes, saying there was a chilly sensation in every part of his body. Baker advised him to put on his cloak, which he did.

Apparently, Murray and Carter appeared at about this time. Wilson told the three of them to go on slowly and he would catch up with them. They walked for a while, then stopped and started to smoke; when Wilson didn't appear they went back to the spot where they had left him, but he was nowhere in sight.

They made an alarm in the neighbourhood and a search party was organized. A large number of people gathered, including women. They made great cries of distress when they heard that Wilson was missing, and went off in all directions to look for him. They searched throughout the night until Saturday morning. One hundred persons were involved, assisted by hog hunters who were familiar with the woods. Several gentlemen came over from Manchester to join the search. The whole neighbourhood turned out; but, in spite of all efforts, Wilson could not be found.

About six days later, on Thursday, June 20, startling news was heard. The Custos of Trelawny, Robert Nunes, had sent out posters authorizing the police and other persons to capture Wilson. The posters were put up in several rural districts and in the towns between Falmouth and Linstead. The Inspectors of Police in Trelawny and St. Ann hired men to search for Wilson, who was described as "the heartless robber of hundreds of poor people". Warrants were also issued for his alleged accomplices: James Stewart, Joseph Stewart, J. Greenwood, Mrs. Maltzan and her son Alexander Dixon.

A reward of fifty pounds was offered:

"*For the apprehension of James Wilson, the Secretary of the Trelawny Savings Bank, who has embezzled eight thousand pounds of the...Bank's money, and has absconded.*"

A letter from Wilson was found, in which he confessed that ambition had led him to become a villain. He had wanted to attain a position similar to "other schemers" in the community, and he had managed to falsify the books of the bank in such a manner "as to prevent detection of his system of robbery". He added in the note that he would not allow himself to be taken alive.

A magistrate, Mr. Justice Davidson, spent most of Wednesday, June 26, investigating a charge against the accomplices: Joseph Stewart, Benjamin Stewart and Thomas Dixon "for conspiring and confederating to secrete and assist in the escape from justice of James Wilson who had, as Secretary of the Trelawny Savings Bank, embezzled the sum of eight thousand pounds". Eight witnesses were examined.

That night the town was aroused by the cry that Wilson had been found at Dry Harbour, by Inspector Hart of the St. Ann police, who was now in consultation with Custos Nunes of Trelawny.

John Castello, Editor of the *Falmouth Post*, hurried to the Custos' house to see Inspector Hart. The inspector told him that Wilson was now within twenty-two miles of Falmouth. He had been seen in Stewart Town on Sunday, June 23, in the company of two persons. One of them had gone with him to Dry Harbour where he had been put in a boat by a man named Seivwright, and taken to the old fort near the town.

Hart went to Dry Harbour and at about 5:30 on Wednesday evening, saw a boy coming from the fort with letters in his hand. He took the letters. There were two of them: one to William Nash, the other to William Knox. The letter to Knox said:-

> *Dear Knox,*
> *I am dying I fear, from hunger and thirst. For God's sake send me some water and some bread, biscuits or Johnny cakes. I have eaten nothing since five Johnny cakes, Monday midday.*

*I want you to hide me a day or two. If you refuse, I am a dead man. I am on my way, only some mountain chaps caught me. One of them takes this.*

*Can't I get in your back store, under your bedroom by ten o' clock tonight? A poor repentant sinner begs you, and as a last recourse. I have been very wrong, and have I not suffered for it! I will try to get Willy to go to Falmouth to try and get a boat to take me to Cuba. I had engaged one to take me to the ship, and failed. Will you see Willy about this?*

*I am in the old Spanish Bull Bay. I mean in the old building near where the guns are. Destroy this. I want to see Willy Nash badly. If this boy can't wait for an answer, give him some water and eatables at once. A bottle of water will do tonight if you can't send more safely, but I feel that I could drink a gallon.*

*Unless you wish me to die and not to have a chance at repentance, hide me among Pimento grains or somewhere, until I can get Willie to…go to Falmouth for a boat to take me to Cuba…I beg and pray you for help in my deep deep distress. God help me.*

The letter to Nash said:-

*Dear Willie,*

*Could you come and see me, or can you send me paper, envelopes and a lead pencil or two; and get Greaves and Seivwright to bring a canoe up to me, near the guns tomorrow afternoon? They are to come to me and leave me after dark, in a place I have in view.*

*I can't account for Seivwright's brother not returning after Monday forenoon. I am starving ever since. I could have got on board so nicely had he brought his canoe. Perhaps the police have taken him up.*

Apparently, the boy who brought the letters thought he had delivered them to Knox. Inspector Hart gave him water and food. He instructed two of his policemen to keep a strict watch on the old fort where Wilson was hiding, then hurried to Falmouth to report to Custos Nunes.

After Nunes heard Hart's report, he asked Inspector Stewart of Falmouth to go to Dry Harbour. Stewart said he couldn't go without receiving permission from Headquarters, but he agreed to send four policemen to assist Hart.

Hart left at midnight and reached Dry Harbour at 4:00 am. There, he encountered four men employed by William Knox, who told him they had been asked to take food and tea to Wilson. Hart and twenty policemen went with the four men to the fort. Hart told them to take the refreshments to Wilson and hold him when he began to drink the tea.

As the thirsty, unsuspecting Wilson started to drink the tea, the police rushed into the fort and handcuffed him. All the surprised Wilson could say was:

"Good God!"

Hart found a revolver and three hundred and ninety-two pounds on Wilson. He ordered ten policemen to take the prisoner to Falmouth. Later, however he got a carriage with a pair of horses, took Wilson into Falmouth himself, and delivered him to the Superintendent of the District Prison.

*The Falmouth Post* said that Wilson had "played the part of a desperate villain, and although there is a general expression of sympathy for the members of his family whom he has affected and disgraced, the whole community which he has victimized will rejoice at his conviction in a court of justice."

It was feared that Wilson's friends might try to rescue him, so he was taken to court handcuffed and in the custody of ten policemen. A large crowd of people followed them. The trial lasted several days. Wilson pleaded guilty and was sentenced to a total of sixteen years Penal Servitude by the Hon. Edward Kemble, on Friday, July 26, 1867. He was taken to the District Prison.

In August, Wilson was put on the one o' clock train, in the custody of Inspector Hart of St. Ann, and transferred to Kingston. He was confined in the Penitentiary. It was done very quietly, and, according to the newspaper, the citizens of Kingston were unaware that "the Trelawny Bank forger" was now in their city.

# DR. VINE AND OTHER CHARACTERS

Because Falmouth was a sea-side town, some amount of boat building went on there, at places like Trelawny Wharf, once owned by John Tharpe. Mr. Philbert and Mr. Robert Huie built boats there for Luke Lazarus, a race horse dealer. One was called "The Trelawny", and there were three Lighters named "The Dee", "The Cynthia May" and "The Fulmar." A jeweller on Market Street named Watson, whose hobby was boating, tried to outdo all others by building a motor-propelled boat. He invited the public, to see him take off. A crowd gathered. Watson started the motor. There was a great deal of noise which was very impressive; but the boat did not move. That was the end of Watson's experiment.

According to Inez Sibley and Jasper O'Gilvie, David Lindo had a drug store at the corner of Water Square. The drug store had a pair of "bow windows and a miniature bay widow". Within them were large two-gallon carboys (glass bottles, enclosed for protection in basketwork or wooden crates) with different coloured liquids: red, blue, amber, yellow and green. This signified that the place was a drug store.

At the rear of the building was an Acetylene Generator, the best form of lighting then in use. Because the store was so colourful and "up to date", it became a gathering place for doctors in the area. The most notorious of these medical men was Dr. Simeon Theophilus Vine.

Vine was the son of a planter and was said to be the grandson of an engineer named Field, who had built the famous landmark in Falmouth known as The Dome. It was constructed in 1810, as part of a foundry. Vine was sent to Edinburgh University in Scotland to study Medicine. His best friend there was Arthur Conan Doyle, who was later to become famous as the creator of the fictional detective, Sherlock Holmes.

As a student at Edinburgh, Vine displayed the "explosive disposition" for which he was to become famous. It was said that every college revolt was started by him, and that he thought nothing of beating up one of the professors. When Conan Doyle began writing his detective stories, he called one of them: *The Mad Student*. The principal character was said to be his student friend : S.T. Vine.

In Falmouth Dr. Vine became known for his use of "crude methods", especially in surgery; but no one dared to protest "unless he or she wanted to be thrown out of his office". One day Vine was in an Operating Room, cutting into an abscess at the sternum of an infant. He was being assisted by the hospital's pharmacist. The father of the infant was also present and began to object to the rough manner in which Vine was performing the operation. Vine immediately lost his temper. He threw away the scalpel he was using and attacked the father. The pharmacist jumped in to try to part the two struggling men. Unfortunately, he stepped hard on the foot of the father and injured it. Apparently that put an end to the fight.

Another time a man went to Vine's office and complained that he had "a "crick neck".

"Try to move your head," said Vine.

"I can only move it this way," the man replied, turning his head to the right.

Vine immediately struck him hard on the face, so that his head flew to the left. The crick neck disappeared at once.

It was a day and age when doctors were few and far between.

It wasn't wise to offend the one in the town who was just around the corner. Apart from not wanting to arouse his temper, patients rarely complained, because Vine charged very little.

The first car that came to Falmouth was brought in by an American. When Dr. Vine saw it parked by the roadside, he went up and started to examine it. The American walked up and asked him what he wanted.

"I am looking at the car," said Vine angrily. "Why shouldn't I? It's in my country."

"Don't interfere with my car," the American insisted.

"Well if you don't like it," roared Vine, "do something about it," and immediately took off his jacket and began rolling up his sleeves. At this stage, it appears that there was some intervention which prevented a fight.

When buses started to run Vine would sometimes take one. If he thought the driver was going too fast he would make a great fuss, and demand that he slow down. People remembered with a smile how he had attempted to grow rice in the swamp around Martha Brae, and how the venture had come to nothing. Vine was described as being slender in build, with a light olive complexion and a sharp-looking face. He sometimes drank hard, and did pretty much as he pleased.

Vine loved to dance and soon earned the reputation for being the worst dancer in Trelawny. Two Trelawny sisters, Ella Louise and Florence Adelaide had vivid memories of trying to avoid him on the dance floor. Ella and Florence were the daughters of John Moore, the Overseer of Swanswick Sugar Estate. John's half brother, Sam, was the owner of Cave Valley Estate. The Moores often travelled to Falmouth to attend balls at the Court House. Dr. Vine was usually there, and for some reason he loved to dance with Ella Louise and Florence Adelaide. He would roam the vast ballroom, looking for them in the crowd of merry-makers. They would see him approaching and try to hide themselves; but sooner or later he would catch up with them.

What was it that made Vine such an atrocious dancer? The Moore sisters said "He exaggerated every step."

In addition to his office and dispensary (pharmacy) he kept a shop where he sometimes spent quite a bit of time relaxing and chatting with customers. He was the family doctor for the Chief Clerk of the Trelawny Parochial Board, William Fitz-Ritson, and it was alleged that he had attempted to instruct the children of the family in the fine art of swearing. One day "a child fell ill and a message was sent to Vine to come at once. A considerable time went by. Vine did not appear. The anxious Chief Clerk went first to the dispensary but Vine was not there. He hurried over to the shop and found Vine standing behind the counter having a leisurely conversation with some of his customers.

Fitz-Ritson, who was a big, powerful man, seized a large cheese knife which was lying nearby and plunged it violently into the wooden counter. Vine instantly recoiled and ran into a back room of the shop.

"Dr. Vine," Fitz-Ritson shouted, "if you don't come to my house at once, and if anything happens to my sick child, I will run this knife into you just as I ran it into the counter." Then he turned and stormed out of the shop.

After a little, Dr. Vine peeped cautiously from behind a door, and enquired of the startled customers if Fitz-Ritson had gone. When they assured him that the outraged Chief Clerk had departed, Vine hurriedly got his instruments and rushed over to the Fitz-Ritson's home. Fortunately, for all, the child recovered.

According to existing records, Fitz-Ritson was the only man that Dr. Vine backed away from. But the doctor had his revenge of a sort. He went to see the Chief Clerk in his office in the Court House one day. They had an argument and the Chief Clerk asked him to leave. Vine strode out of the office in a fury, but, as usual, he was unable to control his fiery tongue. When he got to the bottom of the outside steps of the building, he shouted terrible insults at the Chief Clerk for all to hear.

Fitz-Ritson is alleged to have run out of his office and hurled himself at Vine. Fortunately, one Mr. Arnett was passing by and managed to intervene.

In addition to being Chief Clerk, Fitz-Ritson was Inspector of Poor and Clerk to the Poor House. He was also Secretary of the Falmouth Water Works, Secretary of the Trelawny Parish School Board, Secretary of the Falmouth and Good Hope District School Board, Manager of the Falmouth Government School, Returning Officer for Trelawny, and Parochial Registrar for the Trelawny Taking Census in 1911 and 1921. At the outbreak of World War I, he was made the Parochial Organizing Secretary for the Cycle Scout Corps, guarding the coast line of Trelawny (with himself being the scout for the Falmouth coast). He was the Organizing Secretary for Local Recruitment in the Parish, and Parochial Registrar for registering men for Military Service. Though Trelawny had the smallest population, it took seventh place in the number of men recruited.

In spite of being outstandingly dedicated to public service, Fitz-Ritson's temper could be strikingly short, as in the case of his encounters with Dr. Vine. One day, Mr. Murray, the Town Crier, who was affectionately known as "Turtle", went to see him. Murray was poor and uneducated but he was intelligent and very concerned for the community. He was called Turtle because of his squat, bulky body and short neck. He was disturbed by the fact that when poor people died, they were often buried in a callous, unceremonious manner. So he called on the Chief Clerk to see what could be done.

Turtle and Fitz-Ritson worked out a scheme called the Benefit Burial Society. Membership fee was three pennies per week. If members became ill they would be looked after. If they died, they would be given a "proper" funeral, with marching music and all.

Following up on this worthy initiative, Turtle dropped into Fitz-Ritson's office without an appointment. Fitz-Ritson was very busy and asked him to come back later. Turtle insisted that his business was urgent, and when he was still denied entry, burst into the Chief Clerk's office. Fitz-Ritson was sitting behind his desk.

"I can't see you now, Turtle," he said, "please come back later."

"I have to see you now," Turtle insisted, and refused to leave.

Fitz-Ritson leapt to his feet, wrestled Turtle through the door and along the passageway, and hurled him down the steps. Turtle landed heavily and broke his big toe. However, the two men remained good friends and firm collaborators in the Benefit Burial Society.

Fitz-Ritson was an enthusiastic Methodist Lay Preacher. He was made Circuit Steward in charge of all Methodist churches in the Trelawny circuit. A group of fishermen used to keep their boats on a stretch of open land between the Public Works building and the Court House, where there was a sea wall. On Sunday afternoons, they would gather there to socialize. One Sunday Fitz-Ritson appeared among them and started talking about life and spiritual things. The next Sunday, he re-appeared with Sankey hymn books, and started a sea-side mission among the boats: Bible-reading, hymn-singing, teaching and conducting service.

Fitz-Ritson's enthusiasm often rose to considerable heights when he preached. Speaking in one sermon about women kneading dough, he began to knead imaginary dough on the rostrum. He kneaded so hard that the rostrum began to shake and creak. The lamps on either side were on the point of crashing to the floor. Warning murmurs of alarm rose from the congregation and Fitz-Ritson, alerted to the danger, was forced to stop kneading.

At a concert held to celebrate the end of World War I, Fitz-Ritson sang a patriotic song called *Fight for your King and Country*. As he sang on the platform, he made dramatic fighting movements with his arms. The audience was spellbound. The last line of the song was *Die for your King and*

*Country.* At the end of this line, Fitz-Ritson threw himself flat on his back on the platform, like a man shot dead.

As the platform shook with the impact of his more than two hundred pounds of bodyweight, the people sprang to their feet with cries of horror. They had been so carried away by his performance that they thought for a moment he was dead.

Two other notable Trelawny characters were Lionel Solway Haughton Boothe and Alfred Leopold Delgado. They were good friends. Lionel Boothe was one of three brothers. He had a property called Maxfield near to Merrywood, and became known as "Busha" Boothe. In 1920, Maxfield was referred to as a grazing pen of over one thousand, five hundred acres. Busha Boothe set up house with a black lady who bore him several children. In addition, he had many children by other women; so many that he lost count. In a country which had become infamous for irresponsible fatherhood, Busha Boothe was near to setting some kind of record. Occasionally, when a child with the Boothe look turned up at Maxfield, he would ask:-

*"Which one is your mother?"*

*When he was informed he would generally say:*

*"O yes. I remember her."*

Alfred Leopold Delgado was a Jewish merchant who had a hardware and farm-goods store. He was also a real estate investor, a Justice of the Peace and Chairman of the Trelawny Parochial Board.

One day, Busha Boothe went to Delgado's store to do his weekly shopping. They began to exchange stories and gossip and Delgado said:-

*"Have you heard the latest story in the parish?"*

*"What's that?"* asked Boothe.

> *"The latest story is that there are three Boothe brothers, with distinct characteristics: the eating Boothe, the drinking Boothe and the fornicating Boothe."*

The two men laughed. As the laughter died, Boothe said quietly, with a glint in his eyes:-

> *"I don't have to tell you that there is a story in the parish, which says there is only one Delgado. And that one is the che-eating Delgado."*

It took a moment for that drawn-out word "che-eating" to penetrate Delgado's mind; and when it did, the smile began to fade from his face. But both men remained good friends, and Boothe was one of Delgado's best customers.

Dr. Vine, as usual, seemed to have the final word in the disposition and rating of three of the town's major characters. According to the eccentric and irreverent doctor, the Holy Trinity resided in Falmouth:-

- DELGADO, *Chairman of the Parochial Board was 'god the father,'*
- EWEN, *Custos of the parish was 'god the son,'* and
- FITZ-RITSON, *Chief Clerk of the Board, was ' god the holy ghost.'*

Another outstanding Falmouth personality was Nathaniel Walters, affectionately called "Natty" by everyone. He was the gardener and custodian of "The Park," which stood north-west of the town, on part of the land near the sea that used to be called "Grass Piece".

The Park was enclosed by an ornamental iron fence, and was named Victoria Gardens in honour of Queen Victoria. However, children always referred to it as "Natty Park," because it was presided over by Nathaniel (Natty) Walters, a gentleman with a "green thumb". He planted and tended many rare plants and beautiful flowers, trimmed the hedges and kept the walkways clean.

On Saturdays, people would go to the park to buy flowers. On Sundays, families and couples would stroll through the gardens, and perhaps rest for a while on the benches to enjoy the foliage and the delicate smells of blossoms and blooms. Children would skip and scamper under the trees, being careful not to trample on Natty's plants. Once or twice a year, the West India Regiment band would put on a concert from the bandstand in the centre of the park. It was always sure to draw a crowd.

Natty started work at seven in the morning and continued until six in the evening, or later. He worked seven days a week. He even worked on Christmas. One family, who greatly admired Natty, usually invited him to Christmas dinner; but they had to fit in with his schedule. He told them frankly that he could not come until he had finished work, and had bathed and dressed. So they waited on him. At about six in the evening, Natty, appropriately dressed, would turn up at the residence of his hosts. He would be escorted upstairs to partake of a delayed, but delicious Christmas dinner.

The high wall which protected Natty Park from the direct impact of the sea air, eventually cracked and was demolished. It was replaced by a much lower wall which could not protect the plants from the salt air. The park began to deteriorate.

After forty-five years at the park, Natty retired. It was the final blow. The park disintegrated, and with its disappearance, a vital part of Falmouth was lost.

# **WILLIAM CHIN-SEE**

Another noteworthy Falmouth personality was William Chin-See, who was described by his daughter-in-law (Helen Hu Chin-See) as a man with "a will of iron".

William Chin-See was born in China in about 1866, and came to Jamaica during a period when things were very hard. Plantation owners were still struggling to find cheap labour to work the surviving estates. Chinese workers, experiencing tough conditions in their own country, had acquired the reputation of being able to work very hard for little money. The Jamaican authorities, responding to the labour needs of their still-prestigious planter class, asked the Hong Kong authorities to recruit workers for the estate owners. They were indentured workers, contracted to work for a number of years. Each estate owner would request twenty or thirty, etc; depending on the need.

When the workers landed in Jamaica, they would be taken to Spanish Town. Estate owners would send carts there to pick up their quota. According to Helen Hu Chin-See, that is one reason why the Chinese tend to be found "evenly distributed throughout Jamaica." William Chin-See was one of the indentured workers, and he was taken to either Hampden or Green Park Estate in Trelawny.

The Chinese workers lived in the typical hard, rough conditions which Jamaican sugar workers endured. Unlike their Jamaican counterparts, they were strangers in a strange land, and did not have the benefit of family and community support.

After a hard day's labour in the sun, the workers retired to dark, cramped quarters, badly lit by oil lamps, where they were bitten by mosquitoes.

As a temporary escape, many turned to alcohol, dominoes and whatever women they could find. They fell into debt, and got into the habit of borrowing money from the estate owners "against next year's pay." They sank deeper into debt and were unable to free themselves from their employers because they owed them so much. But William Chin-See sat in the dark at nights, killing mosquitoes and resisting the temptation to find solace in destructive pastimes. At the end of seven years, he was free from his indentureship, owing no man; and, with the money he had saved, was able to launch out upon a new, independent way of life.

He had the experience of planting rice in China, so now he decided to cultivate rice on the flat, swampy Trelawny land. The rice flourished, but when a certain time of year came around, an army of crabs appeared and ate much of the crop.

William Chin-See refused to surrender. He opened a very small shop, selling to poor people. But he knew very little English and had to find a way to communicate with customers. So he put a bamboo stick outside the shop and when customers came, they took the stick and pointed to items on the shelves which they wanted. He would give them and take the "trupence or the quattie," or whatever the price was.

In this unorthodox but businesslike manner, William Chin-See began to prosper. With the passing of the years, he acquired about half the properties in Falmouth's Water Square.

William Chin-See had left his wife behind in China when he came to Jamaica. They were about the same age. Now that he was prospering, he decided to send for her. His friends advised him against doing so. They said she was too old to bear him children and he should send for a younger woman. William Chin-See said that his wife had shared the years of poverty with him, and now she must share his prosperity. He sent for her and she subsequently bore him three children.

By the time William Chin-See was in his fifties, "he was all worn out" by a life of unsparing effort. He died at about the age of fifty-nine; but he left an enduring mark in Falmouth, and he remains in memory as "a man with a will of iron".

# THE COURAGEOUS KNIBB SISTERS

The Polly Knibb School was founded by two sisters: Mary (Polly) and Lillie Knibb. They were the daughters of Edward Knibb, who was a nephew of the great Baptist Missionary and Emancipator, William Knibb. Polly and Lillie were described as "an institution in Falmouth".

A relative, who was a student at the school during its last years, gave a vivid description of the Knibb sisters. They were both very tall. Polly, the elder, was very large, and "wore black velvet bonnets with parrots' feathers on them". Perhaps she got the name Polly from wearing this feathered headgear, which, when tied beneath her chin in a certain manner, gave an indication to her students of the mood she was in.

Lillie was "slender and willowy", with a graceful walk, which her students and relatives liked to watch.

In the 1890s, the school had about twenty boarders and an equal number of day students. These girls were the daughters of *bushas* or estate managers, store keepers, preachers, etc. Discipline at the school was rigid. The girls lived "entirely by clock and rule". The menu was the same each week. On Sundays, the fire in the kitchen was never lighted and the food was served cold: cold corned beef, cold yam or other vegetables, a hunk of dry bread and water. For dessert, cooked prunes one week and apple sauce the following week.

The boarders rose at 6 a.m. dressed, and went downstairs to prayers. Afterwards, they got a "bit of bread", calico tea (half milk and half water) and fruit. Then out into the flag-stoned yard for a study session, which meant walking up and down and around the flower beds, with a book in hand. They had to walk with perfectly straight backs. Any girl seen slouching was given a "back board" to wear, which forced her to maintain an upright posture.

At 8 a.m. the day scholars arrived. Everybody then went into a large room on the first floor which was furnished with long tables and backless benches, which had the effect of encouraging an upright sitting posture. Slates and pencils were brought out and work began. When it was time for Recitation, the girls lined up in front of Miss Lillie with the palms of their hands on their shoulders, and recited portions of the Bible.

Classes in History, Geography, Arithmetic, Spelling, French, Latin and Music (piano) were taught upstairs by Miss Polly. When reciting to Miss Polly, it was impossible to get away with anything, for she could lip-read. Any girl who made a mistake, or who erred in some manner, was sent to stand in a corner with a book on her head. Every time the book fell off, it meant five minutes extra in the corner. On Saturdays, girls who "erred" in anyway were made to walk up and down for ten minutes with a book balanced on the head. Again it was a wonderful way of improving the posture.

Breakfast was served at 11 a.m. and was "always codfish, rice or yam, chochos, etc." Dinner was "mutton, fish, beef, vegetables and fruit". Each afternoon, when school was over and before it was time for dinner, the boarders went upstairs, washed up, and changed into street clothes. Accompanied by Miss Lillie and one other teacher, and wearing hat and gloves, they went for a walk. They walked two by two in lines, and while going through town were not allowed to speak. When they reached the beach, the dock, or the Martha Brae River (depending on the direction of the afternoon's walk), they could break ranks, wander around a bit, and no doubt chat to their hearts' content. On returning to school, they would have dinner, and then study some more, around a huge table at the head of the stairs, until 9pm, when they would go to bed.

On Sundays, the girls marched to the Presbyterian Kirk to attend service. Miss Polly played the organ, and if she happened to disagree with something the minister said in his sermon, she was quite likely to tell him so after the service. Apart from her teaching duties, the dynamic, imposing Miss Polly was the business manager of the establishment, and did the ordering of food, linens, etc. The school was instrumental in building discipline, character and a high sense of self-worth.

The Polly Knibb School was for girls, but at least one small boy apparently attended it for awhile. He was Thomas H. MacDermot, who became a writer and a poet, and is popularly known today as Tom Redcam (which is MacDermot spelt backways). The Jamaica Library Service is now known as the Tom Redcam Library.

Tom Redcam received much of his education in Falmouth, starting at age eight. He attended the Falmouth Academy and then became a student of Miss Lilly and Miss Polly Knibb. Later, he was tutored by ministers of various denominations and by Miss Annie Fray, a granddaughter of William Knibb. Annie's father was a former student of the Calabar Theological College in Trelawny, which had been set up by William Knibb.

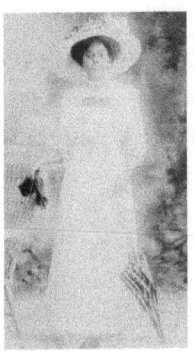

**ELLA LOUISE MOORE**   **FLORENCE ADELAIDE MOORE**

Doctor Vine's reluctant dancing partners, Ella Louise Moore and Florence Adelaide Moore, also attended the Polly Knibb School, as did Henrietta Brown, who later married the Chief Clerk of the Falmouth Parochial Board. Henrietta wrote a letter to the *Jamaica Times* newspaper on October 3, 1914, which was published on Saturday, October 10. In it, she said:

*The news has just reached me of the death of our dear Miss (Polly) Knibb; she has not long survived her sister Miss Lilly, who went home just under a year ago. This brings to an end the earthly life and service of these two sainted women, but it by no means ends the holy and lofty influence which contact with them was sure to impart and which will without doubt go on forever...*

*For are there not scattered over Jamaica and in many foreign countries too, hundreds of women who today thank God that they had...the advantage of being taught at the Seminary of the Misses Knibb, and so enjoying the blessing of their strong and ennobling character, and their industrious and holy lives....*

*Falmouth was the poorer when these ladies found it necessary to leave for Kingston, and everyone who had the opportunity went to say good-bye to Miss Polly and Miss Lilly.*

*Now they are gone. All the girls (now women) they have influenced for half a century will remember them with only deep and tender affection.....*

*I am writing to put forward a suggestion...My proposal is that all the pupils who have passed through the school of the Misses Knibb contribute four or five shillings towards a suitable Memorial Tablet to be erected over their resting place, for I presume Miss Polly has been laid to rest beside the remains of Miss Lilly.*

Henrietta suggested that a small committee of former students living in Kingston could find out the whereabouts of former students, prepare and issue a circular, act as treasurers, select a suitable tablet with an appropriate inscription and plan a short ceremony. Henrietta concluded by saying:

> *The strenuous work and labour of love of these two saintly and exemplary women, deserve this and much more too. I feel sure that those who have benefitted by, and cherished fond and tender recollections of these Dear women will rally to this deserving call. My sisters and myself will be willing to give a small subscription and do anything possible towards the plan.*

The Knibb sisters were remarkable in many ways. For one thing, they engaged in a lot of charitable work. Mr. Delgado, owner of the most popular and important store (Emporium) in the town, invariably put them in touch with needy cases.

The school was virtually closed down in the late 1870s over an incident involving colour discrimination. The parents of some of the students demanded that two newly-enrolled dark-skinned girls (daughters of a Baptist minister and a Presbyterian minister) be removed from the school. Miss Polly and Miss Lillie refused. As a result, the other students were withdrawn by their outraged parents and the school collapsed.

Because of this disgraceful incident, the Baptists started a school in 1880, dedicated to the education of girls, regardless of class or colour. The first teacher was a relative of Miss Polly and Miss Lillie, and the school eventually developed into Westwood High School, located at Stewart Town in Trelawny.

Miss Polly and Miss Lillie managed to revive their school shortly after.

# THE SILVER CUP OF DANIEL O'GILVIE

In 1918, the Inspector of Police for Trelawny, John H. Charley, went bird shooting with Jose Charley of Hanover and Dennis Lynch, Superintendent of the Public Works Department. Inspector Charley was to celebrate the second anniversary of his son's birth later that day.

The three men travelled nine miles from Falmouth to a pond at Wakefield, which was also called the Weston Favel Lake. Birds swarmed about the pond and the water was full of duck weed. When they arrived, Inspector Charley went to the east side of the pond and his two companions went to the north.

Birds flew over and the inspector fired. A bird fell into the water, some distance from where he was standing. He stripped off his clothes but kept on his slippers, and began wading through the duck weed towards the place where the bird had fallen.

"Don't go in there," said Dennis Lynch, "the duck weeds are fearful."

"This part is quite clear," the inspector replied, and started swimming out. Shortly after, he seemed to be struggling to move.

"O Lord, help me, help me," he shouted.

"I'm going down, I'm drowning. My feet are tied up with duck weed."

Three times the inspector went down and rose again, shouting for help. He went down a fourth time and did not reappear. People ran up but no one would go in.

Lynch and Jose Charley jumped into their car and raced to Falmouth to report what had happened. A party, headed by Dr. G.P. Campbell, hurried from Falmouth to the lake.

Hundreds of people gathered and the police tried to get volunteers to go in. Money was offered but no one would volunteer. The risk was too great. Several people had drowned in the lake, and just a fortnight before, a boy had met his death there.

At this point, Daniel Leopold O'Gilvie, Assistant Inspector of Poor, employed to the Parochial Board, arrived on the scene. He immediately volunteered to go in.

A bamboo raft was built. O'Gilvie got on the raft and paddled out to the spot where the inspector had disappeared. He dived and began searching. The spectators watched anxiously each time he went down, wondering if he would rise again. Within half an hour O'Gilvie found the body, in about ten feet of water. He brought it ashore. It was put on a stretcher and taken to Falmouth where an autopsy was performed.

The body was later taken to Kingston to be buried at the Half-Way-Tree Cemetery. The funeral procession left from the residence of Mr. & Mrs. E. W. Lucie-Smith on Leinster Road. When the procession reached Half-Way-Tree, the West India Regiment Band, which was waiting at the clock tower, began to play. The band accompanied the procession to the cemetery.

Back in Falmouth, William Fitz-Ritson, Chief Clerk of the Trelawny Parochial Board, formally brought O'Gilvie's brave deed to the Board's attention. The Board unanimously agreed that representation should be made to the goverment for some recognition to be given to O'Gilvie. Fitz-Ritson wrote the Colonial Secretary on March 20, saying:-

*The Board believes that an act of this kind, evincing such pluck and unselfishness, and high regard for public duty, deserves to be publicly recognized in some tangible and befitting manner...and directs me to request you to bring the matter to the attention of His Excellency, the Governor.*

On March 23, the acting Assistant Colonial Secretary, D. M. Wortley, replied to say that it was the intention of goverment to present Mr. O'Gilvie with a silver cup, suitably engraved, in recognition of his courageous conduct.

Seven days later, Inspector Charley's widow, Dorothy, wrote O'Gilvie:-

*It must have been a most difficult and dangerous task,"* she said, *"and only a brave man could have done it. I shall never forget, that, had it not been for you, my husband's body might never have been rescued and brought back to me...I also feel sure, had you been with him at the time, I should never have lost him.*

*I will be sure to tell his parents of the debt of gratitude we all owe you, which I am sure will never be forgotten by any of us, nor by our baby son, when he grows older and learns."*

The Governor had to leave the island before the presentation. But on May 14, Mr. Wortley wrote to the Custos of Trelawny, Hon. H. Jarrett Kerr, saying that prior to the governor's departure, he had approved the presentation of a silver cup to O'Gilvie. Since he was unable to present it personally, he was asking the Custos to do so in his stead, at a public function.

On June 13, after the regular meeting of the Trelawny Parochial Board, a special function was held to present the cup. In attendance were Custos Jarrett Kerr; Hon. Guy S. Ewen MLC; Hon. C.W. Hewitt MLC for Hanover; A. L. Delgado Chairman of the Board; J.H. Clerk Vice Chairman; Revs J.T.H. Chandler; R.L. Knight; M.M. Lumsden; Messrs George Taylor; P.E.F. Robertson; N Wooler; S.H. Stewart; D.A. Delgado; George McGrath; W. Scholefield; H.P. Sewell; John Stockhausen; Joseph Stockhausen; F.L. Harris; Rev. Scrivener Lea; Messrs A.E. Muschett; Archie Campbell; H. Levy; W.J. Whiting; D.N. Ingram and W. Fitz-Ritson. A squad of police under Sergeant Major Brown was also present.

Chairman Delgado related the sad event of Inspector Charley's death and the brave recovery of his body by Mr. O'Gilvie. The various letters dealing with the matter were read, and the silver cup was filled with champagne by Mr. H. Percy Sewell.

The cup was then presented to Mr. O'Gilvie, and the hope was expressed that he would retain it as a souvenir and hand it down to his family. Members of the O'Gilvie family, who were present, sipped champagne from the cup.

Mr. S. Stewart, who was a schoolmate of O'Gilvie, then told some boyhood stories. He remembered that the sea was their place of recreation, and O'Gilvie and his elder brother, George, would swim far out into the harbour, where others didn't have the courage to go. The O'Gilvie brothers had taught many boys to swim, said Stewart, and he was not surprised that Daniel had retained his boyhood daring and had made "History for Trelawny".

In replying, O'Gilvie regretted that he had not been at the pond in time to make an effort to save Inspector Charley; for he had cared for him very much. He said he would treasure both the cup and Mrs. Charley's letter, and hand both down as heirlooms.

In 1931, Dan O'Gilvie succeeded Fitz-Ritson as Chief Clerk of the Trelawny Parochial Board.

# THE POOR HOUSE AND MATRON MARION

In 1918/1919, the Falmouth Poor House got a new Matron. She was one of the daughters of the Chief Clerk of the Parochial Board. They called her Marion, and she was only twenty years old.

At the age of sixteen, Marion ran away from Westwood High School. She took shorthand lessons to become a secretary but gave up after three evening classes. She was just too full of soaring thoughts to sit still. Her favourite character in literature was "Joe", the irrepressible heroine of Louisa May Alcott's popular novel, *Little Women*.

Marion seemed happiest when she had lots of things to do, so her bewildered father put her in charge of his large household at New Haven, about three miles from Falmouth in the district of Granville. There, among other things, she defeated a determined praedial thief by tying a bottle of blue liquid to a tree. That was big magic, and the thief never returned.

Marion was made Superintendent of the Granville Sunday school. She read and told Bible stories to the village children, and became such an excellent story-teller that the parents began attending Sunday School just to hear her. Her big dream was to study nursing at Tuskegee University in the United States. She imagined herself walking through the streets of Falmouth in a stiff, white uniform carrying a black bag. The fare to America in those days was only five pounds, but her father thought that Tuskegee was too far and wouldn't let her go. She was bitterly disappointed.

She had grown into a handsome, imposing young woman, about five feet eight inches tall, with grey-green eyes, a straight back and a well developed figure. She had many admirers, but fell in love with a young man who was determined to go to the United States to seek his fortune. So she lost him.

Marion was suffering from a broken heart when the position of Matron at the Poor House became vacant. Her father, the Chief Clerk, got the job for her. In a way, it was close enough to the profession of nursing which she had hoped to study. And she would be wearing a stiff, white uniform.

The poor, the sick, the unwashed and the neglected awaited her as she stepped boldly through the gates of the Poor House on her first day on the job; a bright-eyed young woman of twenty.

There were over seventy people at the Poor House, and twenty-year old Marion soon began to regard them as her "children". It was fortunate for her that she had had the experience of running the New Haven household. The first task for the day was to get breakfast for the inmates. This generally consisted of a pint of bush tea and a loaf of bread which Marion issued to each one with her own hands to make sure they got it; for apparently there were cases where somebody would make off with somebody else's breakfast. Those who weren't well enough to eat the regulation breakfast were given something else.

After breakfast, Marion listened to the various complaints of the inmates, then gave instructions to the nurses and porters about things that must be attended to before the doctor made his regular morning visit between ten and eleven o'clock. When he arrived, Marion would meet him, "all stiff and pretty" in her immaculate white uniform. Then she would make "the rounds" with him from bed to bed, and receive instructions on how to treat some of the inmates who were unwell. Those that she could not manage were turned over to the dispenser (pharmacist) at the Falmouth Hospital next door. A new dispenser had arrived two weeks after Marion took up duties as Matron.

After the doctor's departure, it would be time for lunch. The food would have been given to the cooks after breakfast and would by now be ready. Once again, Marion would serve the meal herself, sharing it out and handing it through a kitchen window.

The women would be served first. When she was ready, Marion would say: "Come on, women," and they would come hurrying out of their wards, some with sticks to help them along, to get their "pudding pans of grub and mugs of soup". Then it would be the turn of the men, some of them eyeing the grub in the pudding pans "most greedily," but the majority quite satisfied because the Matron had shared it herself.

When lunch was finished, the pudding pans and spoons would be washed and put away, and tobacco and pipes would be issued to those who smoked and were well enough to do so. The inmates would recline all over the compound, and chat and smoke and take it easy. Persons who were sick would be served meals in bed, with food specially ordered by the doctor. Marion would always visit them to see that all was well. Then she would retire to her quarters for a rest until about four o'clock, when it would be time to see to the preparation of supper.

Supper was another cooked meal, and was served between five and six, in the same manner as the other meals. Just before six o'clock, the day nurses would collect the pipes and hand them over to the night nurses, as smoking in bed was not allowed. That would be the end of the day, and the inmates would shuffle off peacefully to bed.

Washing had to be given out and checked every day; and on Fridays, when everything was clean and neatly folded, Matron would check each item after lunch, and have them all put away in the store room. In addition, there were children of school age who had to be sent to the government school every day; abandoned babies who were bottle-fed and kept in a separate ward, and insane people who had not yet "committed" themselves, and could therefore not be sent to a Mental Home.

One day, a mad woman attacked Marion and chopped her on the head. She went to her father to tell him about it and was most distressed when he only said: "Report it to the Police," and never even glanced at her cut forehead.

If the women made trouble and started to fight among themselves, Marion would charge into them with a "supple jack" (a kind of cane that could be used as a whip), and promptly restore order.

When some of the men began to feel better and could move around with vigour, they would feel they no longer had to obey the rules. But Marion would quickly restore discipline. One of her favourite methods of punishment for the unruly was confinement in bed and a diet of "*Black Pap*" served twice a day. "*Black Pap*" was made of corn starch and a small amount of sugar. No milk was put in it. Two days of Black Pap was usually enough to break the spirit of the most rebellious.

Marion's chief helper and handyman was a huge man named George Henry Bailey. Marion described him as having "two left feet". Among other things he used to chop wood for the kitchen and when she called out to him (always by his full name: "George Henry Bailey", he would always reply:

"Yes, Missis; coming, Missis; coming please Ma'm."

Then he would come up the walk-way "as fast as his two left feet would allow him."

In spite of her no-nonsense attitude, the inmates loved Marion. When she entered the men's ward in the mornings and said: "Good morning men," they would reply in unison! "Good morning, Matron. God bless you." Sometimes, when she went to the bed-sides of the women, they would put their arms around her and say: "God bless you." Some dying inmates would ask for her, and the night nurse would come to her quarters and wake her, sometimes at midnight.

She would hurry to the ward and put her hand on the dying person, and would hear a whispered: "God bless you, Matty."

MATRON MARION
of the Falmouth Poor House

Marion's greatest test came when a murderer suffering from tuberculosis was brought in one day. He was supposed to have been hanged, but instead he was sent back to the parish of his birth (Trelawny) and placed in the Poor House, because he was so ill. Everybody was afraid of h im, including the nurses, and no one wanted to go near him. He had to be put behind a screen. Matron Marion herself was afraid, but since nobody would attend to him, she had to feed him herself. Everyday when she approached the screen behind which the dread-looking murderer lay, she would say in a clear voice: "Compose yourself. Your Matron is coming."

The part about composing yourself was probably as much for her benefit as his. Having made this introduction, she would approach his bed and feed him.

The best time of the year at the Poor House was Christmas. The Falmouth merchants would give Marion donations of either money or groceries. A big Christmas tree would be set up in the compound and the town band would be on hand to play. Presents would be put on the tree and every patient would be given one. Ministers from various churches would attend, along with the Chairman and Members of the Parochial Board, friends and relatives of the inmates, and some of the town folk. There would be plenty to eat and drink and lots of music.

Those of the inmates who were able to, would attend the five o'clock Christmas morning service and then promenade about the town afterwards.

To enrich the spiritual life of the inmates, a minister from one of the churches would hold a service in the male ward every Thursday morning; and everyone would gather there to worship, including the Matron. Most of these activities were introduced by Marion during her stay at the Poor House, and many of them were allowed to fall away after she left. She never got to Tuskegee to study nursing, but in a way, her dream of walking through the streets of Falmouth in a stiff white uniform carrying a black bag was fulfilled during her term of office as matron. She was always a "people person", instinctively knowing how to enrich the lives of others and creating an atmosphere where they could feel wanted and at home.

Marion resigned from her job at the Poor House in 1923, when she got married and left Trelawny.

# 'CLASSIC' CHARLIE - THE SHARK KILLER

The Government Pharmacist, who took up duties in Falmouth at around the beginning of 1919, was an unusual character. In later years, admiring colleagues referred to him as a classic pharmacist. Observing his consistently high performance over a period of time, they would come to the conclusion that he was among the best pharmacist in Jamaica, if not the best.

In the early days, students of Pharmacy in Jamaica had to learn to make powders, pills, ointment, cream, gargles, mouthwashes, disinfectants and all kinds of pharmaceuticals and medicines. They had to dress wounds, set broken bones, etc. Classic as we will now call him (although he had not yet earned the title) became an expert in all the mysteries of the pharmaceutical professions. In addition, he made fine wines, cordials, exotic perfumes etc. He was called Dispenser, a sort of Colonial name, which adequately masked the value of the profession and thus justified a relatively small salary.

Classic had many interesting past times. He caught butterflies in big white nets and preserved them. He gathered certain leaves and flowers and press them between the pages of books to preserve them. He played a good game of cricket and was a useful batsman. As a dancer he was far from being perfect, his movements were definitely not smooth and rhythmic. In-fact, they were rather jerky. But he was not as terrible a dancer as the notorious Dr. Vine.

Perhaps Classic's greatest asset was his beautiful tenor voice, he sang at numerous concerts, and was invited to private gatherings at homes to sing for families. When he sang such songs as "I'll take you home again, Kathleen", and "In the Gloaming, oh my darling", tears would come to the eyes of hardened, sophisticated men-of-the world.

Classic described Falmouth as quiet and picturesque. There was not an overabundance of work, and he found plenty of time for his favourite diversions. As a part of his work he had to make frequent trips into the interior of Trelawny with a medical officer. Up in the wild back-country, there was a tedious job to be done; treating yaws and inoculating children against small pox. At the end of the long days, the medical officer and Classic would tramp wearily back to town, with their bodies and spirits in-dire need of refreshment. They usually headed straight for the nearest shop, for a welcome snack of tinned fish, water crackers, pepper and rum.

Two of Classic's other interests were swimming and fishing. The house where he was quartered stood near the sea shore. At eight o'clock one night, he threw out a line and tied it to a stake a few feet behind the house. The next morning, when he went out and picked up the line, he felt there was something on it and began pulling in. Whatever was on the line was heavy, and he had to use a lot of strength. A terrific struggle took place between Classic and the fish. When he finally managed to pull it out of the water, it turned out to be a shark, seven feet long. By this time, people hearing of the catch, began running towards the water front. Classic, impressed by the strength and size of the catch, killed it immediately. A crowd had now gathered at the scene, to view the monster of the deep; which had been heroically captured and slain by Classic.

Unfortunately, the monster turned out to be a nurse shark, which, despite its seven foot length was quite harmless. The crowd took it all in. The tremendous excitement, generated by the terrific encounter between Classic and the seemingly dangerous sea creature, quietly disappeared into the cool morning air. There were smiles and a few chuckles.

Many years later, Classic was elevated to the most senior pharmaceutical post in Jamaica: Island Medical Store Keeper (otherwise called Superintendent of medical stores or Director of Medical Stores.) He was the first Jamaican to be permanently appointed to that post. But those who knew him best remembered him as Classic Charlie Robinson, the Shark Killer of Falmouth, a man who brought tears to the eyes when he sang "I'll take you home again Kathleen".

# THE GHOST OF PHILIP FITZ-RITSON

Philip Morrison Fitz-Ritson was one of ten children, born a twin with his sister Leonie. His mother, Henrietta, and his seven sisters thought he was the handsomest man in Falmouth, if not in the entire Jamaica.

Phil (as he was called) was six-feet tall, well built, straight, muscular and weighed about 175 pounds. He never took a music lesson, but he only had to hear a tune, and he could go to the piano and play it perfectly. He was a kind of saint, and everybody loved him. But this is not to say that he did not have his share of boyhood pranks.

Once he went with some friends to Half Moon Bay for a swim. They buried their clothes in the sand to safeguard them from being stolen. When they were ready to leave they could not remember where they had buried the clothes. So they waited until night, then ran home naked as fast as they could.

Another time, during a very dull church service, Phil was observed crawling down an aisle on all fours during prayers, and escaping through a side door.

Phil liked to keep fit. He was chopping wood with an axe one day on his family's 14-acre property at New Haven, when a chip flew up and damaged one eye. After a while it seemed to heal. When World War I broke out in 1914, Phil was 19 years old. He was said to be the first one in Falmouth to volunteer for the Jamaican War Contingent to go overseas to fight the Germans. Inspired by his father, he had a burning desire to offer his life in service to a noble cause. Following his example the young men of Falmouth hastened to join; but to everyone's surprise, Phil was turned down, because of his damaged eye.

Phil was stunned. He tried again but was once more rejected; forced to stand on the sidelines and watch his contemporaries getting ready for the great adventure. Shamefully cast aside; excluded from the mightiest challenge of his generation.

Heart-broken Phil decided to go to England, hoping to be accepted there. He only got as far as Panama where he remained for two and a half years, working in the Canal Zone. One day he heard that Jamaicans in Panama were being recruited for the Jamaican War Contingent. He returned home at once. At his family's New Haven home, he spent six weeks exercising and making himself as fit as possible. Then, for the third time, he took the physical examination. This time he passed, perhaps because by 1917, the requirements were not as strict.

Phil was elated. He enlisted as a common soldier on October 10, 1917, at the age of twenty-two and was attached to the garrison at Port Royal. Some of his acquaintances had enlisted as officers. When they saw the new recruit they either ignored him or treated him like a stranger. Their rebuff did not discourage him but acted as a spur.

Among his batch-mates Phil immediately emerged as a leader. If he was going to church meetings the other chaps were going too. If he was entering the Athletic Competition the other fellows were entering too. Fortunately Phil would lead no one into evil ways, for there was no evil in him. One boyhood friend said: He was perfect and set an example to all his friends. He would not do anything behind his father's back that his father would be ashamed of. Phil saw the war in the noblest light: as a struggle to secure a free world for free people to live in; something to cheerfully give up one's life for.

On November 1, 1917, about twenty-two days after enlisting, Phil was made a Lance Corporal. On November 9, he won first prize in an athletic competition. Six days later he was promoted to Sergeant. On November 18, he was designated Orderly Sergeant for his company. On December 1, he was made Acting Company Quartermaster Sergeant. He had taken to military life as naturally as a duck takes to water. When he returned to Falmouth on December 20, on leave for the Christmas holidays, he looked every inch the soldier, everyone was proud of him.

There was a comic song at the time which Phil played and sang on his visit:
> *When you see me on parade,*
> *With my dim and dusty blade,*
> *Showing off my figure,*
> *Full of vim and vigour.*

Phil also played at a sold-out concert at the Court House on Thursday, December 27, 1917. On January 7, 1918 Phil reported back to the garrison at Port Royal. On March 30, he was promoted to Company Quartermaster Sergeant; on May 8 promoted to Acting Sergeant-Major; and on June 24, he attained the rank of Second Lieutenant.

When Phil appeared in his Lieutenant's gear, some of his officer friends who had ignored him before came up to shake hands. At that moment, Phil committed what might be called the only "mean" act of his life. He put his hands behind him, turned his back and walked away.

Phil's promotion was received with jubilation. He was deeply appreciated because of the keen interest he had taken in the spiritual and moral welfare of his comrades. Rev. Arthur Kirby referred to him as "the best type of a West Indian: generous, polite, calm, gentlemanly and yet resolute, prompt, reliable in every way."

Second Lieutenant R.E. Kearney of Goodwin Park, Kingston said that Phil had "the rarest and finest of all things, a capacity for sincerity. Whatever he did was solid and real and well done...He was the finest type of Jamaican and one who gives us hopes of this little island." Second

Lieutenant Vernon Lee of Moneague described Phil as "a master of everything he put his hands to, and a wonderful example."

Phil was eagerly poised to leave for France, but fate denied him that "supreme privilege." The Germans were in full retreat. The war was drawing to a close. The Jamaican War Contingent was disbanded, and on October 7, 1918, all officers were given leave. Phil suddenly found that the prize for which he had worked so hard was snatched away from his reaching hands. He must have been gripped by severe frustration and depression.

In the meantime, the dread disease called Spanish Influenza had broken out in many parts of the world. It swept through the ranks of the young and the strong and destroyed tens of thousands. In October the newspapers reported that the disease was spreading to too many places in Jamaica. On Wednesday, October 22, there were nearly two hundred cases in and around Falmouth, and two hundred and fifty in and around Clarke's Town, ten miles away. There was no "drug preventive" for the disease and no specific remedy. Victims were put to bed immediately and kept there.

Stores, shops, wharfs and offices "were depleted of staff". Fresh cases were reported everyday. Dr. G.P. Campbell, the District Medical Officer of Health, was ill and confined to his residence. Dr. S.T. Vine, "though ailing, was moving about, but with difficulty." In normal times, the hospital was considered crowded if it had twenty patients. Now it was accommodating "upwards of sixty." The National School premises were fitted out to receive patients.

Phil, in a bewildering state of unwanted idleness, was asked to assist with the establishment of temporary "Flu" hospitals in Trelawny. He jumped at the opportunity. People remembered him going busily up and down in his khaki uniform, a picture of health and vigour. Just the sight of him was reassuring.

On Monday morning, November 11, news came that Germany had surrendered unconditionally. There were resounding shouts in Falmouth of "Old England forever" and "hurrah for the allies". The joy felt by all "was beyond description. That night the YMCA band "paraded the streets of Falmouth with patriotic music, stopping at each home from which a soldier had been taken and giving the relatives the benefit of the music." Later in the night, the band was invited to the Northside Club, where the gentlemen most liberally refreshed the boys at intervals. Coming on to midnight the band departed, "with every man singing God Save Our Gracious King."

It appears there was a strange sadness in at least one heart. At midnight on November 20, in the midst of the excitement, Phil suddenly became ill. His illness struck just when the epidemic appeared to be on the wane. On November 22, a newspaper reported that "in a few days time the Bunker's Hill Hospital will be closed for want of patients."

Phil took to bed at New Haven. No one was unduly worried. Everybody felt that if anyone could shake off that dreadful malady, and arise whole and healthy, then certainly that one was Phil. Phil began to burn. The doctor laboured furiously. The family hovered around, doing whatever they could. Phil burned and burned with fever. Finally, the doctor announced that in addition to Spanish Influenza, Phil had Black Water Fever. Things looked grim. Black Water Fever was a killer.

An official directive was sent forth at around this time, saying that all officers of the disbanded Jamaican War Contingent must relinquish their commissions on November 30. It was all over. On Monday morning, December 2, 1918, with his mother and father on either side of his bed and the rest of the family nearby, someone said: "How do you feel, Phil?"

"Like a burning star," Phil replied; and those were his last words. At 8:30 am, Phil went burning into eternity. He was 23. One of his sisters pricked the sole of his foot with a safety pin to make sure he was dead, as Phil had had a fear of being buried alive.

When Phil's mother, Henrietta, realized he was dead, she fell wailing to the floor, and rolled in agony from one side of the room to the other, back and forth, weeping uncontrollably. Her beautiful son was gone. So intense was her anguish that her health was undermined from that day, Phil's twin, Leonie, wished to die and be with him.

The funeral procession left New Heaven at 8:30 am on Tuesday, December 3. Mourners joined the procession at every point. When it neared the town, another large company came out to swell the advancing throng. The whole of Market Street was densely packed. Business was suspended as stores, shops and offices were closed. One old woman was heard to say: "Nobody left in their house this morning."

When the procession reached the Methodist Church it was already full. There was hardly any standing room. Three clergymen officiated including the Baptist Rev. R.A.L Knight.

Phil's death brought reactions from all parts of the island, even from people who did not know him. Millions of young men had died because of the war, but the singling out of Phil seemed relevant and appropriate. "We all ask why" said Vernon Lee. "It's all a mystery, too deep for us to understand."

Lester G.F. Kirkcaldy wrote:- "We enlisted about the same time...I can hardly believe that the young, strong, healthy, jolly Fitz of our acquaintance is now gone... The Fitz that I knew, though but for one short year; the Fitz of the simple faith in the Christ that he loved, followed and encouraged his comrades to follow.

Phil's parents said:- "He was solicitous of our comfort...sparing no pains to show his gratitude and love to his sisters) he was watchful, loving and protective, anxious to do little services of love for each one. To his younger brother, he tendered example and counsel, ever creating a spirit of comradeship and manliness for their emulation."

The poet J.E. Clare McFarlane, who did not know Phil, wrote:-

> "Thy gleam hath shone afar, thy message given,
> Oh youth! The proof is that I know thee not;
> Though thou are gone thy deeds are not forgot,
> And mark in glorious trail thy flight to Heaven.
> I knew thee not but these I recognize;
> Beyond the gloomy silence of the grave
> They link thee to thy country in whose eyes.
> Thou hast done well – Thanks unto Him Who gave."

By nature Phil was not the warrior who slays. His nature was to protect, love, guide and inspire. There was a curious parallel in his family heritage. His ancestor (unknown to him) who brought the Ritson name to Falmouth, was also an army lieutenant. He was in the 55th Regiment of Foot and died in 1806 of yellow fever (it is said) while serving with the regiment in Jamaica.

In 1937, Phil's mother, Henrietta, was sitting in a rocking chair on her verandah with her grandchildren about her. She was wearing a locket with a picture of Phil on a chain around her neck. One of her grandchildren, Beverly Aarons, pointed behind Henrietta and said: "Grandma, the man in the picture you are wearing is standing behind you."

Henrietta did not look, but her face became illumined by a bright smile. She chuckled as she rocked gently, back and forth.

# THE COURT HOUSE BURNS

The first Court House in Falmouth was at the corner of Duke and Princess streets, where the Methodist Church now stands. The premises were acquired from William Danny in 1795, and occupied in May 1796, when the Vestry (as the Parochial Board was then called) held its first meeting in Falmouth.

Eighteen years later, on Monday, April 11, 1814, a special meeting of the Vestry was called, and it was resolved to build a new Court House in Water Square, at a cost not exceeding ten thousand pounds. On July 24, 1815, the representatives of Edward Moulton Barrett were paid one thousand pounds for land at the "Old Fort" (near Water Square) on which to build a new Court House. Work began soon after, and dragged on for nearly two years. In the end, the cost was about fourteen thousand pounds. Fittings, furnishings and the cost of the land brought the total to about twenty thousand pounds.

The new Court House was finished and occupied on April 7, 1817. It was regarded as the best in the island. No expense was spared in the furnishing and general equipment. All the furniture was made from mahogany and cedar. The building was eighty square feet, and about thirty feet high. The cut stone walls were two and a half feet thick; the upper and lower floors each had eighteen tall windows, and the four stone columns supporting the front porch, were about two feet in diameter.

The ballroom was the most splendid part of the Court House. It was eighty feet long and thirty feet wide. Instead of the usual mouldings, the room had artistic "gold, gilt decorations" on three sides. Suspended from the ceiling were three sparkling chandeliers, crowded with candles. They were made of cut glass and burnished brass, showing a blend of "the rose, thistle and shamrock." On very special occasions, great scarlet tapestries were mounted on the walls.

Portraits of two 'popular' governors hung in the ballroom: Major General Sir John Keane and Sir Charles Metcalfe. Sir John Keane was Lieutenant-Governor in 1827. He was a keen sportsman and spent many weeks in Trelawny each year, fishing and shooting. He became personally acquainted with the Trelawny elite and they admired him so much that they acquired a large portrait of him and hung it in the ballroom. The portrait was a replica of one belonging to the Keane family, which had been painted by Sir Martin Archer Shee.

Sir Charles Metcalfe became governor in 1839 and took a great interest in the sugar and rum industry. This earned him the affection of the Trelawny planters.

When the British government put a heavy duty on sugar in 1840, Sir Charles went to England and successfully presented the case of the Jamaican planters to the government. To show their gratitude, the planters raised money to acquire a portrait of him, which was hung in the ballroom along with the one of Sir John. The portrait was painted in 1846 by G. Bradish.

The Court House was the heart and nerve centre of Falmouth, and of the whole parish of Trelawny. The most important functions for the highest officials and the most glittering social events were held at the Court House. Balls, concerts, plays, readings, lectures, displays of magic, etc, drew eager crowds to the Court House. In times of crisis (the Sam Sharpe Rebellion), people looked to the Court House, since it was the seat of parish administration. William Knibb and his fellow missionaries were detained in the ballroom in 1832.

The police station was in front on the ground floor of the Court House, and the lock-up was behind it. On the eastern side was the office of the Chief Clerk of the Parochial Board, and close by was the office of the Superintendent of Roads and Works. Sanitary conveniences were also on the ground floor.

Upstairs on the eastern side was the Great Ballroom with its tall windows, in which the Parochial Board held its meetings. On the western side was the Courtroom, and at the northern end the Court's office. The judge's room was in between the Courtroom and the ballroom. When concerts and plays were held in the ballroom, the judge's office was used as a dressing room by artists and actors.

The Court House was indeed a place of many and varied activities. Attending a function there, gave one a feeling of privilege.

Invariably, it was a time for dressing up in one's best clothes; of seeing and being seen; of showing-off whatever one had to show-off: an attractive wife and daughters, a new carriage, or a brand new suit, imported straight from London. To stride up the imposing entrance steps, mount the broad stairs and sweep into the ballroom, was like going to Buckingham Palace; especially if the Governor was the honoured guest.

On Thursday, August 12, 1926, the Parochial Board held one of their usual meetings in the ballroom. It was to be their last in that particular setting. At two o'clock on the morning of Thursday, August 19, the inhabitants of Falmouth were awakened by the cry of "fire".

The fire started in the cellar of a dry goods store called the "Temple of Fashion"; a very old, wooden building owned and occupied by Ethelred D. Arscott. The fire spread to the first floor, then to the second and third. The police and the antiquated fire engine rushed to the scene, but the old, wooden building was already burning fiercely. The flames leapt across the street and set fire to another three storey building which was the residence of Josephine

DeLisser. The water pressure was too low to help the firefighters. In addition to that, as they struggled frantically with the fire hose, it broke, due to dry rot. Giant tongues of flame leapt into the sky, and shot out in all directions, beating back the puny efforts of the fire fighters. The DeLisser house was consumed.

People gathered nearby, despite the unbearable heat. Board members and employees of the Board were there. The Court House was across the street from Arscott's place. They watched in apprehension as a land breeze blew the sparks over and drove the heat on to the Court House. An urgent message was sent to Montego Bay asking for help; but long before help arrived, the porch of the Court House caught fire. The fire fighters dashed across and were working to put out the flames when a shout went up that the south side was ablaze.

A great cry of dismay arose from the crowd as flames took hold of the roof. Someone got hold of a small "chemical" extinguisher but it was totally useless against the raging fire.

John Warburton, Keeper of the Chandeliers and other treasures, ran into the Court House and brought out the life-size portraits of Sir John Keane and Sir Charles Metcalfe. Members of the Board and employees of the Courts office entered the building and brought out records and valuable books. The old piano was hauled out, together with many old mahogany chairs and tables and nearly all the couches. Only a portion of one chandelier was rescued.

Men, women and children "vied with each other to save the pride of Trelawny and the monument of its glorious past". It was all largely in vain. The splendid Jamaican Coat of Arms, the wall decorations, the antique scarlet tapestries went up in smoke and flames. The only thing that saved the walls was the heavy plastering of lime mortar on the inside, which absorbed the heat.

At six in the morning, the Montego Bay Merryweather fire engine, which was in 'tip top' shape, clanged up to the scene; but it was much too late. Major destruction had already been done. The fire was finally put out shortly before mid-day, thanks to the "splendid work" of the Montego Bay firemen.

At half past three on the afternoon of August 19, the day of the fire, an emergency meeting of the Board was called. It was held in a house on the north-eastern corner of Duke and Market streets, owned by William Fitz-Ritson, Clerk of the Board. A report was made on the destruction caused by the fire.

Apart from the Court House, the store premises of E.D. Arscott and the residence and store of Josephine DeLisser; the other places destroyed were: the Episcopalian Rectory, the residence and store of Chin-See Brothers, the residence of Eugenia Cunningham, outbuildings of the Presbyterian Manse, the Lock-up store of Delgado Brothers, the residence of Florence Walsh, and part of two premises owned by Daniel O'Gilvie, who had pulled Inspector Charley's body from Western Favel pond in 1918.

Telegrams and messages of sympathy poured in from Governor Edward Stubbs, Colonial Secretary Jelf, and other prominent people.

The rebuilding of the Falmouth Court House was completed towards the end of 1929. The Board formally

**THE COURT HOUSE**

took over from the contractors on November 28. It met for the first time in the refurbished building on December 12. On April 10 the following year (1930), the Board appointed a committee to make arrangements for the formal opening of the Court House. The date was to be May 16, if the Governor found it convenient.

In spite of all the restoration efforts, the aura of majesty and magic was never quite recaptured. The link with roots and heritage, the historical and symbolic significance, had lost their strength. The glittering chandeliers were gone forever. Electricity was in, and candles had become obsolete. Complex electric-light fixtures were installed. The tapestries were never replaced; and with the passing of the years, the life-size portraits of Keane and Metcalfe mysteriously vanished. The graceful roof line of the Court House had been replaced with a less aesthetic design in the rebuilding.

In a way, the burning of the Court House symbolized the decay of Falmouth. The decay had started about seventy years before, almost unnoticed.

In the 1850s, when the Jamaican sugar industry was in serious decline, the industry remained vibrant in Trelawny, which was the chief sugar-producing parish at the time. Falmouth was full of life and activities of all sorts. The waterfront was alive with industrious workers. Apart from Kingston, Falmouth had the most external trade. Falmouth took second place to none in terms of its sporting activities, the often exciting and imaginative cultural events which centred on its impressive Court House; and the many families of merchants, professional and country gentry which graced the town on social occasions.

Perhaps the challenge to Falmouth's supremacy began when the railway, which was opened in November, 1845, was extended to Montego Bay in 1895. Montego Bay began seriously to rival Falmouth as a distribution centre. Towards the end of the 19th Century, ships became bigger, too big in some cases, for the Falmouth facilities.

Rocks which had been an impediment in the harbour were blasted away, and the channel was dredged. This did not significantly halt the decline of Falmouth as a port. After the 1907 earthquake, Kingston arose, stronger than ever, as a centre for the importation of goods. By that time, the sugar industry in Trelawny was hardly any better than elsewhere. As steamships took over from sailing ships, and loading methods shifted from manual to the steam derrick, shipping activities were concentrated more and more in Kingston and Montego Bay.

Employment at the port of Falmouth declined. The town's vitality rapidly seeped away. Many of the families that had been associated with the town, in a vigorous way, vanished from the scene.

# **EPILOGUE**

Falmouth never recovered its glory as a thriving commercial centre. The town's decline is starkly seen through the eyes of the Lazarus sisters, Vera and Lally.

There were seven children in the Lazarus family: Willie, Vera, Ouida, Lucille, Lally (Ulalia), Louis and Sam. Their father, Samuel Lazarus, was from a Jewish family, but they were Roman Catholic. There was no Roman Catholic church in the town, however. Father Becker, the priest, from Montego Bay, would come up once a month, rent a room in a building near the Grass Piece, and there hold services and give communion.

At first, Samuel Lazarus worked at Trelawny Wharf, owned by Kerr-Jarrett. Later, he acquired his own wharf, near the place known as the Rock. He called it Union Wharf. Samuel Lazarus bought sugar, rum, fustic, logwood, annatto, pimento and other commodities for sale to ships, most of which came from Denmark. He used to entertain the captains and officers at his home.

Vernon Arnett married Lucille Lazarus. His brother Harry, who was once Chairman of the Trelawny Parochial Board, owned a combination garage and gas station near the Court House. When Harry wasn't there, Lucille's younger sister, Lally, at the age of fourteen, ran the gas station. Harry would give her an open cheque to pay for gas deliveries and other expenses.

In later years, Vera and Lally recalled that there was very little to do in Falmouth when they were growing up.

Now and then, they would go to a function at the Court House. Occasionally, they went to the cinema run by Mass Johnny Cadien. Mostly, they just went for walks. When there was a Pocomania meeting on one of the back streets, they would stand on the bank of the road and watch the "Poco People".

Antonio, a Syrian, had a store with very nice cloth. Vera and Lally and their other sisters would go there to shop. Their father, Samuel Lazarus, used to go with Antonio to Dan O'Gilvie's house once a week to play whist. That was a high point in their limited social calendar.

Like many young Falmouthians, the Lazarus boys left the town after they grew up. Willie went to Cuba. Louis went to Miami, became captain of a ship, and took on his brother Sam as his engineer. Louis eventually went to Mexico and entered the shrimping business.

It was Custos Roy B. Barrett who reminded us of some who kept Falmouth going after it slipped from its eminent position. Individuals such as:-

*Alexander Dunbar* (Mass Jim) Goldsmith; manufacturer of earrings, bracelets, bangles, belt-buckles, chains and rings; repairer of watches and clocks, who kept the public clocks going in the squares of Falmouth, Wakefield and Duncans. Mass Jim was also Attendant Officer for the Falmouth Primary School. He made sure that students got to school on time and brought in truants by force to face the headmaster. He served for years as Deacon of the William Knibb Memorial Baptist Church and gave all his children names from the Bible.

*Ernest Augustus Nunes* (1906-1973) Tinsmith; manufacturer of dish covers, pots, pans, measures, funnels, graters, bird cages and lamps. He soldered gutters on houses and motor car radiators, made and fitted catchment pipes from houses to domestic water tanks; repaired just about everything made of tin. For relaxation, he spent many hours fishing at sea.

*James Conrod Leopold Walker,* Cabinetmaker; upholsterer and wheelwright; maker of fine furniture (four-poster beds, tables, chairs) with his father's home-made wooden lathe; upholsterer of chairs and settees; making cart wheels and fitting on the iron tyres produced by the blacksmith.

***Howard Stanley Barrett,*** Blacksmith; sharpening pick-axes, agricultural forks, crow bars, chisels, punches, horse shoes, etc; shoeing horses and mules and fitting handles to clothes irons; cutting bottles to make drinking glasses and vases; making iron tyres for buggies and mule carts. Mr. Barrett was a devout Baptist, a Deacon and a Lay Preacher.

***Dorothy Nugent,*** Teacher/Typist. She taught young girls to type and do shorthand in the evenings at her home in Market Street. She was Superintendent of the William Knibb Memorial Baptist Church Sunday School. For over forty years, she prepared children for the annual anniversary programme, the Christmas Morning Concerts, etc; teaching them to bow gracefully and to pronounce every word audibly. Miss Nugent also played the organ.

***Luther Campbell,*** Decorator, promoter and artist. He was an ardent churchman who could read music and play the organ. He made posters, banners and wreaths; and decorated churches and homes for special occasions. Mr. Campbell promoted and acted in many "surprise concerts", and was Superintendent of the local Christian Endeavour Encampment.

***The Garth brothers (Robert and John),*** sailors and fishermen; owners of canoes, yachts and coasting vessels. Robert worked all around Jamaica on boats, and handled cargoes of lumber, logwood, fustic and sugar. John repaired and built boats at Rio Bueno, Falmouth and Montego Bay. He had an intimate knowledge of all the harbours from St. Ann's Bay to Lucea. Both Robert and John were cricketers and were famous story tellers of local lore and sea adventures.

***Benjamin Powell,*** Educator. An outstanding educator in the latter part of the 19th Century was Benjamin Powell of the National School, which was famous on the North side. Fitz-Ritson was one of Powell's students from the latter half of the 1870s into the 1880s. He remembered Powell as a very tall, dignified, courteous gentleman who was always smartly dressed. A role model. Daniel O'Gilvie, who came along later, remembered him as "Old P," on whom the boys played practical jokes. Once they put a "Flying Horse" in his chair. Another time they plastered it with cobbler wax, which caused his pants to stick to the seat and tear away when he started to rise. Mr. Powell died about the year 1909.

A few years before Mr. Powell's death, the National School was closed and a Government school was opened at the former Fort Balcarres. Two of the outstanding teachers there were Ralph Hammond and his wife, Ruth. Headmaster Ralph Hammond served from 1921 to 1952, and was active in social and church work. Ruth Hammond served even longer: 1921 to 1957; thirty-six years.

## HONOURABLE MENTION

### *The Most Honourable Hugh Shearer*
The third Prime Minister of Jamaica, The Most Honourable Hugh Lawson Shearer, was born on May 18, 1923 at Martha Brae village, which was the first capital of Trelawny. He was also a student of the Barracks Government School in Falmouth.

### *The Honourable Usain Bolt*
Usain Bolt, (nick-named lighting Bolt) was born on August 21, 1986, in Sherwood Content, Trelawny. He is a Jamaican sprinter and a three-time World and Olympic medallist. He has direct family connections with Falmouth; his maternal grandmother Marcia Davis was born in Falmouth and his maternal grandfather worked with the Trelawny Parish Council that was housed at the historic Court House building. His mother, Jennifer, was born at 26 Cornwall Street in Falmouth. Bolt's connections with Falmouth could very well be seen as a signal of an illustrious re-birth for the historic town of Falmouth - capital of the parish Trelawny.

# BIBLIOGRAPHY

1. *Journals of the Assembly of Jamaica.*
2. *History of the Parish of St. James in Jamaica* – John Roby.
3. *An abstract of the Government of Jamaica* – Sir Thomas Lynch.
4. *Narrative of Certain Events Connected With The Late Disturbances in Jamaica* – Thomas Abbott.
5. *Lights and Shadows of Jamaican History* – Richard Hill.
6. *The History of Jamaica* – W.I. Gardiner.
7. *The Daily Gleaner (1918), (1926).*
8. *The Royal Gazette.*
9. *The Falmouth Post & Ja General Advertiser 1835-1874.*
10. *Jamaica as It Was, Is, and Could Be* – Bernard Senior.
11. *History of Jamaica* – Edward Long.
12. *Facts and Documents Connected With The Late Insurrection* – William Knibb.
13. *Governors of Jamaica in the First Half of the 18$^{th}$ Century* – Frank Cundall.
14. *Lives of the Lindsays, Vol. 2.*
15. *Letter to Geoff Pinto from Mrs. Cicely Knibb Allen (1971).*
16. *Fitz-Ritson Family Papers.*
17. *History of the Parish of Trelawny* – Dan L. O'Gilvie.
18. *History of the Falmouth Court House* – Dan L. O'Gilvie.
19. *Annals of Jamaica* – G.W. Bridges.
20. *Death Struggles of Slavery* – Rev Henry Bleby.
21. *Reminiscences of A Scottish Gentleman* – Philo Scotus (Philip Barrington Ainslie).
22. *The Handbook of Jamaica; 1885 – 1886; 1920.*
23. *Proceedings of the House of Assembly, Relative to the Maroons (1796).*
24. *Private Letter Re- Maroon War, and Report of Colonel Walpole (1796)* – A. L. Balcarres (Ms 613).
25. *Letter to Superiors in London re – Jamaica Militia – May 3, 1795* – Earl Balcarres (Ms 606).

26. *A Brief Account of the Present Style of the Negroes in Trelawny* – James Stewart of Trelawny
27. *The Voice of Jubilee* – John Clarke.
28. *Extracts from Trelawny Militia Records 1828-1832* – John Kitchen.
29. *The Craftsmen of Falmouth, and Profiles* – Roy Barrett (contained in the *Souvenir Handbook of the Trelawny Cultural Foundation*).
30. *Selections from Browning* – H. A. Needham.

# Index

## A

Accompong 6, 13
Ainslie, Philip Barrington 34, 35, 36
Alhambra 83
Annatto 14, 161,
Arscott, Ethelred 156, 157, 158
Ashenheim, Lewis (Dr.) 84
Atterbury, John 92

## B

Baptist Herald 76
Baptist Missionary Society 46, 54
Baptist War 44
Baptists 44, 45, 47, 53, 71, 72, 107, 133
Barrett Browning, Elizabeth 20, 21
Barrett, Edward Moulton 17, 18, 19, 20, 21, 151
Barrett, George Goodin 19
Barrett Hall 19
Barrett, Hearcey 17, 22
Barrett, Samuel 17
Barrett Town 18, 21, 24
Beecher Stowe, Harriet 20
Biggs, Joseph 8, 9
Black Shots 10
Bleby, Henry (Rev.) 55
Bolt, Usain 164
Bonaparte, Napoleon 36
Boothe, Lionel 123
Bounty Hall 52
Breach of Promise of Marriage 92
Britain 2, 38, 54
Browning, Robert 20, 21
Brunswick 3
Buckingham Palace 156
Buie, Theodore 98, 101

## C

Cadien, Johnny (Lieutenant-Colonel) 48

Cadien, William (Colonel) 42
Cambridge Estates 47
Canada 7, 14, 164
Carrickfoyle 52
Castello, John 68, 75, 76, 114
Charles II 1, 17, 33
Charles Town 52
Chippenham 26
Cholera 81
Christmas 77, 83, 107, 109, 125
Chryster, John (Lieutenant) 40
Cinema 162
Cinnamon Hill 17, 19
Coffee 9, 14, 28, 29
Cornwall Chronicle 76
Cornwall Courier 76
Cornwall Gazette 76
Coromantees 8
Cotton, Willoughby (Sir) 48
Coultart, James (Reverend) 46
Coxheath Pen 7, 9
Cudjoe 5, 6, 58
Cuffee 7, 8, 11, 12

# D

Davidson, Harry (Hon.) 92, 114
Delgado, Alfred Leopold 123
Delgado, Charles 100
Delisser, George 100
DeLisser, John 101
Delisser, Josephine 156, 157, 158
Dickson, William 34
Doig, Paul (Captain) 49, 61, 66
Doyle, Conan 118
Dry Harbour 14, 114, 116
Duckworth, John (Admiral) 35
Duke Street 79, 80, 95
Duncans 2, 79, 84, 90

# E

Edward Trelawny 3, 5
Emancipation 26, 66, 107, 111
England 14, 15, 19, 21, 24, 25, 27, 34, 44, 46, 47, 54, 58, 59, 94, 134, 148, 151, 155

Eyre, Dunlop 104
Eyre, Edward John (Lieutenant Governor) 87, 100, 101, 104, 105

# F

Falmouth Gazette 76
Falmouth Parish Church 14, 96
Falmouth Post 66, 101, 103, 111, 114, 116, 165
Fitz-Ritson, William 57, 120, 121, 122, 123, 124, 125, 135, 136
Fontabelle, The 11, 95, 96, 97
Fort Balcarres 32, 34, 36, 161
France 21, 34, 36
Frater, William (Custos) 70, 59
Fray, Annie 131
French Scare, The 32, 40
Furness, Allan 23, 25, 26

# G

George II 2
Gilbourne, Henry 101, 102, 103
Good Hope Estate 22, 23, 24, 25, 26
Gordon, George William 107, 109
Grant, John Peter (Sir) 109
Guthrie, Archibald 34

# H

Halifax 14
Hall, James (Sergeant) 12
Henry, John 76
Hill, Janet 92
History of the Parish of Trelawny 95
Horse Racing 85

# I

Irving, James (Custos) 10

# J

Journal of Kingston 84

# K

Keane, John (Sir) 155, 157
Kearns, Henry 34
Kew, Thomas 8

## K

Kingston 37, 45, 52, 53, 84, 87, 107, 110, 111, 116
Knibb, Edward 129
Knibb, Lillie 129
Knibb, Mary (Polly) 129, 131
Knibb, William 124, 131, 132, 152, 165
Knox, William 114, 116

## L

Leile, George 44
Logwood 28, 162
Longden, John 40
Lucea 32, 33, 37, 39, 72, 94

## M

Magotty Estate 111
Mahogany Hall 11
Mandingoes 8
Mango 29, 90
Mann, James 47
Maroon War 10, 11, 12, 33
Martha Brae 2, 3, 4, 15, 18, 22, 78, 81, 84, 119, 130
McGhie, James 7, 12
Medina 94, 95, 110
Merrywood 24, 26, 123
Metcalfe, Charles (Sir) 72, 123, 155, 157
Methodists 46, 53,
Miller, William 61, 62, 63, 65, 66, 67
Montego Bay 2, 5, 14, 32, 33, 34, 38, 47, 50, 52, 53, 56, 69, 70, 84, 157, 160, 158
Moore, Ella Louise 132
Moore, Florence Adelaide 131
Moore, John 119
Moore Town 52
Moulton, Charles 19

## N

Nova Scotia 7
Nugent (Lady) 25
Nugent, Dorothy 163
Nugent, George (General) 25, 33, 34, 35
Nunes, Ernest Augustus 159
Nunes, M.A. 101

Nunes, Robert (Custos) 105, 110, 113, 116
Nunes, Theodore 83

## O

O'Gilvie, Daniel 134, 158, 164
Othello, The 95

## P

Page, Ann 40
Palmetto Point 18
Pantrepant 11, 24, 46
Paulett, Henry 8, 10
Persian Wheel 15, 79
Pharmacy 144
Pigs 5, 79, 90
Pimento 14, 115, 163
Polly Knibb School, The 129, 131
Polydore 7, 8, 11, 13
Port Antonio 39, 52
Port Royal 32, 34, 60, 148, 149
Portland Point 37
Potosi 24, 26

## Q

Quadrille 79
Queen Victoria 94, 110, 124

## R

Red Hill House 8
Reeves, Samuel 18
Reid, Catherine 58, 60, 62, 63
Reid, Mary 59, 61, 62, 65
Reid, Thomas 58, 60, 62, 63
Reid, William 58
Retirement Estate 36
Ridgeland 46
Rio Bueno 54, 95
Robinson, Charlie 146
Robinson, Crusoe 22
Royal Gazette 37, 41

## S

Savanna-la-Mar 3, 32, 33

## S

Second Breakfast 9, 29
Selkirk, Alexander 22
Sharpe, Samuel 47, 49, 55
Shearer, Hugh 164
Shee, Martin Archer (Sir) 155
Sierra Leone 7
Spanish Town 2, 23, 39, 43, 49, 107, 126
Springfield Pen 93
St. Ann 2, 62, 73, 87, 99, 110, 111, 113, 114, 116, 162
Steel, Alexander 8, 10, 11
Stewart Town 47, 54, 72, 114, 133
Summer Hill Pens 26
Swanswick Sugar Estate 119
Sylvester, John 18

## T

Taylor, Simon 25
Tharpe, John 6, 14, 18, 22, 23, 24, 25, 26
Top Hill 24, 26
Trelawny Advance 76

## V

Vere 17
Vine, Simeon Theophilus 117, 118, 119, 120, 144

## W

Wakefield 102, 103, 162
Wales 2, 24, 26
Warburton, John 158
Warren, John 40
West India Regiments 89
Westmoreland 2, 46, 47
Wiles Town 2
Wilson, James 113
Windsor Pen 8, 11, 26
Withywood 17

## Y

Yellow Fever 32, 45, 152

www.ingramcontent.com/pod-product-compliance
Lightning Source LLC
Chambersburg PA
CBHW032118090426
42743CB00007B/387